Animal Sizes

One of these symbols is shown with each animal. It shows you at a glance how big the animal is likely to be. All measurements describe the length of the animal from the tip of its nose to the end of its tail.

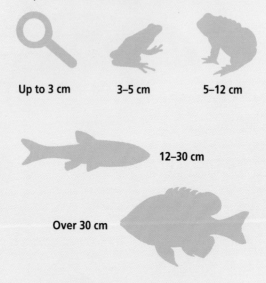

Up to 3 cm   **3–5 cm**   **5–12 cm**

12–30 cm

Over 30 cm

For snakes, the measurements are shown by the symbols below, also from the tip of the snake's nose to the end of its tail.

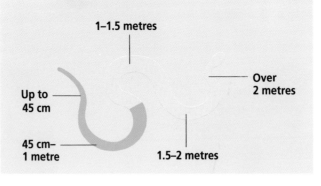

1–1.5 metres

Over 2 metres

Up to 45 cm

45 cm– 1 metre   **1.5–2 metres**

FRESHWATER LIFE

OF GREAT BRITAIN & EUROPE

Susan McKeever

CONSULTANT
Dr Frances Dipper

DRAGON'S WORLD

CHILDREN'S BOOKS

Conservation

Every freshwater animal, from the terrapin to the flatworm, is closely linked to its surroundings. It feeds on other animals or plants and makes its home in a pond, lake, fast-running stream, slow-running river or in wetlands. Many animals prefer particular kinds of climate and landscape. As you learn about a habitat, you will get to know which plants and animals you can expect to find there.

Many of these habitats have been damaged or destroyed by industry and its pollution. People are draining wetlands – like flood plains, marshes and swamps – because they are good places to farm once the water has gone. Some freshwater animals are in danger of disappearing altogether – they are often protected by law.

On page 78, you will find the names of some organizations who campaign for the protection of particular animals and habitats. By joining them and supporting their efforts, you can help to preserve our animals and their habitats.

Countryside Code

1 **Always go collecting with an adult** and always stay close and within sight.
2 **Leave any snakes that you find alone** – they may attack you if frightened.
3 **Leave their nests or dens untouched**.
4 **Treat all freshwater creatures with care** – many can be killed by rough handling.
5 **Ask permission** before exploring or crossing private property.
6 **Keep to footpaths** as much as possible.
7 **Leave fence gates as you find them.**
8 **Take your litter home** with you.
9 **Ask your parents not to light fires** except in fire places in special picnic areas.

Dragon's World Ltd
Limpsfield
Surrey RH8 0DY
Great Britain

First published by Dragon's World Ltd, 1995

© Dragon's World Ltd, 1995
© Text Dragon's World Ltd, 1995
© Species illustrations Individual artists, 1995
© Other illustrations Dragon's World Ltd, 1995

Species illustrations by Bob Bampton, Jim Channell and Colin Newman, all of Bernard Thornton Artists, London.
Habitat paintings by Mike Saunders; headbands by Antonia Phillips; lifecycle and activities illustrations by Mr Gay Galsworthy.

Editor   Diana Briscoe
Designer   James Lawrence
Design Assistants   Victoria Furbisher
                      Karen Ferguson
Art Director   John Strange
Editorial Director   Pippa Rubinstein

British Library
Cataloguing in Publication Data
The catalogue record for this book is available from the British Library.

ISBN 1 85028 294 3

Typeset in Frutiger Light and Novarese Bold by Dragon's World Ltd.
Printed in Slovenia.

Contents

What Could I See?

From quiet ponds and peaceful lakes to rushing mountain streams and steaming swamps, freshwater areas are alive with animals. Water reptiles, like turtles, and amphibians, such as frogs, spend part of their time on land and part in the water. They have lungs and must come to the surface to breathe.

Some water snails have simple lungs and can live in still ponds where there is not much oxygen. Many insects start life in the water, then change into adults that live on land. But most other water animals, like fish, breathe using gills and will quickly die if taken out of the water.

This book will make it easier for you to identify all these water creatures in two ways. Firstly, it shows you only the animals that you are most likely to see. Secondly, it puts them in groups according to the habitat, or type of fresh water, where you are most likely to see them. But remember that many animals will be found in more than one habitat.

Body-changing insects

Some freshwater creatures undergo a change of form that is called metamorphosis.

Dragonflies begin their lives as eggs laid on a water plant by an adult. The eggs hatch into larvae called nymphs, which then live underwater for several years, hiding among the plants, and catching other animals for food.

Eventually, they crawl out of the water and change into adult dragonflies – they have wings, and can't live in the water.

This is called incomplete metamorphosis, because the young don't look that different to the adults. Stoneflies, mayflies, alderflies, and damselflies lead similar lives.

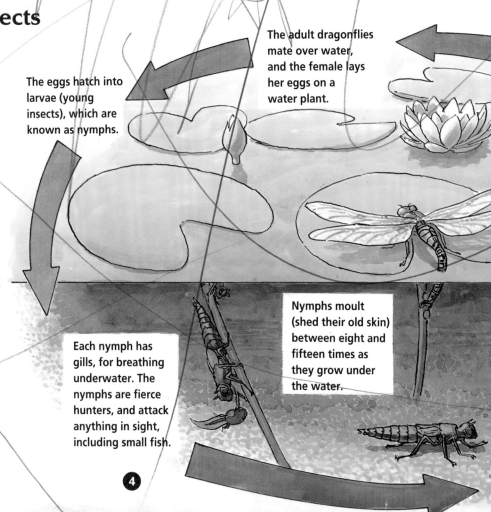

The eggs hatch into larvae (young insects), which are known as nymphs.

The adult dragonflies mate over water, and the female lays her eggs on a water plant.

Nymphs moult (shed their old skin) between eight and fifteen times as they grow under the water.

Each nymph has gills, for breathing underwater. The nymphs are fierce hunters, and attack anything in sight, including small fish.

How to use this book

To identify an animal that you don't recognize, like the two animals shown here, follow these steps:

1 **Decide what habitat you are in.** If you're unsure about this, read the descriptions at the start of each section to see which one fits best. Each habitat has a different picture band heading and these are shown below.

2 **Decide what sort of animal it is.** Is it a reptile or an amphibian, a fish or a mollusc, or something else entirely? Look at the descriptions on pages 6–7 to find out. For example, the Freshwater Shrimp (left and page 73) is a crustacean. Each animal is identified by a special sizing symbol (see the front of the book to view them).

3 **Look through the pages of animals with your habitat picture band at the top.** The picture and information given for each animal will help you to identify it.

4 **If you can't find the animal there,** look through the other sections. Animals move around, and you may see them in more than one habitat. You will find the frog (above right) is a Common Frog (see page 11).

5 **If you still can't find the animal,** you may need to look in a larger field guide (see page 78 for some suggestions). You may have spotted a very rare creature!

Finally, the nymph crawls up a plant stem into the air, and moults for a final time. Out crawls the adult dragonfly, with its brightly coloured body. It waits for its wings to dry, then flies off, a land-based insect.

Watch for empty skins attached to waterplants

Top-of-page picture bands

This book is divided into different freshwater habitats. Each habitat (type of countryside) has a different picture band at the top of the page. These are shown below.

Found Almost Everywhere

Ponds & Lakes

Marshes & Floodplains

Slow Rivers & Canals

Fast Streams & Rivers

What To Look For

Reptiles

Terrapins, snakes, and lizards are all reptiles. Lizards live on land and are not covered in this book. Reptiles have skin covered in scales, or hard plates and shields. They have claws on their toes.

Amphibians

Frogs, toads, newts, and salamanders are all amphibians. They have moist skin with no scales. They do not have claws on their toes. They lay jelly-like eggs in water which hatch into tadpoles.

Fish

It is usually easy to recognize a fish. However, be careful not to mistake eels for water snakes. Some fish have very strange shapes. Look for the number and position of the fins, especially those on the back which are called the dorsal fins.

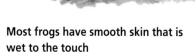

Sunfish have one long fin, spiny in front and soft at the back

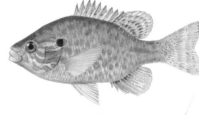

Most frogs have smooth skin that is wet to the touch

Toads have tough, warty skin that is dry to the touch

Eels have one long fin

Perch and darters have two fins, close together

Trout have two fins, one large, one tiny

Minnows have one short fin

Newts and salamanders have smooth skin; most have stout front and back legs of equal size. The belly (underneath) is a different colour to the back

Molluscs

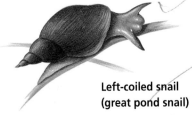

**Left-coiled snail
(great pond snail)**

**Right-coiled snail
(amber snail)**

Two shells (bivalve – river pearl mussel)

All molluscs are soft-bodied animals, and most have a shell. Animals with one shell are called gastropods. Those with two hinged shells are called bivalves. When you see a water snail, check whether it coils to the left or right. Hold the shell upright, with the aperture facing you and follow the coil with your finger.

Crustaceans

Crustaceans have a hard, plated skin, long feelers for finding food, and many pairs of jointed legs. As they grow, they must moult their skin and grow a bigger one. Crayfish, shrimps and prawns are all crustaceans.

Insect larvae

Blackfly larva

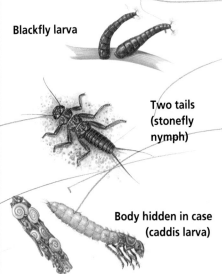

**Two tails
(stonefly
nymph)**

**Body hidden in case
(caddis larva)**

Most of the insect larvae in this book are nymphs. They have bodies that are divided into three parts: head, middle (thorax), and rear (abdomen). There are three pairs of jointed legs on the thorax. There are no legs on the abdomen though some have many pairs of feathery gills – try to count these.

A fly larva looks very different to a nymph. It has a small body divided into segments often with tufts of hair, and a small head.

Worms have no legs and no hard skin or shell. They are usually long and thin. Flatworms have flat, soft bodies and glide over rocks. A true worm's body is divided into segments, and there is no obvious head. A leech's body is divided into segments. There are suckers at both ends, but they are difficult to see.

Worms & worm-like animals

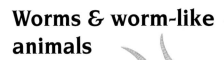

Found Almost Everywhere

Some water animals don't seem to mind where they live. They can be found in streams, rivers, ponds, lakes, bogs and marshes, or even in your garden or in a park. Many of these creatures are also very wide-ranging. You may spot them throughout much of Europe, and even in other parts of the northern hemisphere if you should take a holiday in North America.

You will notice that the only snakes to be found in this book come in this section. This is because these snakes prefer to live near water, but as they only spend part of their time actually in the water, it doesn't matter whether it is a still pond or a fast-running stream.

Some of these animals are also able to survive in waters that have been slightly polluted by nitrates (from farm fertilizers) or by sewage or industrial waste. Very few animals can survive in heavily polluted water, but the worms on pages 14–15 can endure more than most other freshwater animals.

This picture shows eight animals from this book; see how many you can identify.

European Eel, Edible Frog, Perch, Wandering Snail, Grass Snake, Three-spined Sticklebacks, Common Toad, Square-tailed Worm.

Reptiles & Amphibians

Viperine Snake

This snake is so called because its markings look like those of a viper. It is brown or grey, with a broad head and a zigzag row of stripes down its back. If threatened, it will rear up like a viper and strike at its attacker. Luckily it is not venomous. The Viperine Snake lives in or near ponds, rivers and mountain streams, where it feeds on fish and amphibians. It is also known as the Water Snake.

Group: Colubrid Snakes (Colubridae) – Size: Up to 100 cm long
Distribution: Iberian peninsula (Spain and Portugal), Balearic Islands and Sardinia

Green Toad

A colourful sight, the Green Toad has a dark green pattern and red bumps on a light background. It lives near many different types of water, and can often be seen on warm nights near houses and near streets. It feeds mainly on insects, which it often waits for by street lights. Males, which are smaller than females, make a sound like the trilling of a canary during the breeding season.

Group: Typical Toads (Bufonidae)
Size: Up to 10 cm long
Distribution: Central and southern Europe, but not Iberian peninsula, British Isles, Scandinavia and most of France

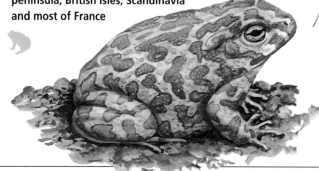

Dice Snake

The Dice Snake spends most of its time in shallow water, where it lies in wait for fish, its main food. It has a narrow, pointed head, and may be brown, grey or green, with dark spots. Underneath, it may be white, yellow, pink or red in colour. It is almost impossible to tell apart from the Viperine Snake – luckily their distribution hardly overlaps. In winter, the Dice Snake comes on to land to hibernate in holes in the ground.

Group: Colubrid Snakes (Colubridae)
Size: Up to 150 cm long
Distribution: Southeast Europe from Italy to Ukraine

Grass Snake

This harmless snake is the most widespread of all European snakes. Its colour is a variable dark brown or green. But it is easily recognized by the bright yellow or white collar with a black border, just behind the head. As its name suggests, the Grass Snake is often found in damp grass, but it hunts mostly near water. It feeds mostly on frogs and toads, but will sometimes eat worms, fish and small mammals. You won't see Grass Snakes in the winter, as they hibernate.

Group: Colubrid Snakes (Colubridae)
Size: Up to about 150 cm long
Distribution: Throughout Europe, except Ireland

Edible Frog

This frog has a pointed snout and is usually grass green to brown with dark markings. A light green stripe often runs down the middle of its back. It never has a dark 'mask' like the Common Frog. It lives in ponds and lakes and, during the winter, hibernates in the mud on the bottom. Favourite foods are insects and slugs. On warm nights, listen for the call of Edible Frogs, which is a growl-like croak.

Group: Green Frogs (Ranidae) – Size: Up to 12 cm long
Distribution: Whole of Europe, except Iberian peninsula and northern Scandinavia. Only a few isolated colonies in southern Britain

Common or Grass Frog

This frog lives in a variety of habitats. In spring it prefers ponds and lakes where it lays its eggs. For the rest of the year it can be found in damp woodlands, marshy meadows, gardens and even high up mountains. It has smooth skin, which is pale with dark markings, but its colour varies greatly. A good way to recognize it is by the dark 'mask' behind each eye, which extends to its front legs. The Common Frog feeds on insects and worms, and hibernates in the mud on the bottom of the pond. Its croak is a very quiet, purring sound.

Group: Brown Frogs (Ranidae)
Size: Up to 10 cm long
Distribution: Most of Europe, but not most of Iberia, Italy and southern Balkans

Fishes & Molluscs

Fingernail Clams

Also called Orb-shell Cockles, these bivalves are yellowish or greyish brown and rounded, but are slightly bigger than Pea Clams. They burrow into the bottom of various freshwater habitats. Young ones may clamber about on water plants. If you collect some and put them into water, you may see the two siphon tubes and the strong foot.

Group: Orb Mussels (Sphaeriidae)
Size: Up to 1. 5 cm
Distribution: Widespread throughout Europe

Pea Clams

Also called Pea-shell Cockles, these little creatures have shells in two parts, so they are bivalves. The shells are yellowish or buff in colour, and rounded in shape. They can be found in many watery habitats, even water troughs, and sometimes burrow into gravel or sand at the bottom. They are difficult to tell from Fingernail Clams. Left in a bowl of water, they may send out two short, joined siphon tubes, through which they draw in water.

Group: Orb Mussels (Sphaeriidae) – Size: Up to 1 cm
Distribution: Widespread throughout Europe

Roach

The Roach is one of the commonest freshwater fishes. It has a small head, and a deep body with bright silvery sides. All the fins are reddish except for the single, brownish back fin and tail. Look carefully at the eyes which are a strong red in adults. Roach live in shoals in a wide variety of lowland freshwater habitats. They feed on many different bottom-living animals such as worms, insect larvae and snails. They also swallow a lot of mud. Females lay their sticky eggs in underwater weed beds.

Group: Carps (Cyprinidae) – Size: Very variable; normally up to 25 cm; exceptionally 50 cm long
Distribution: Widely distributed throughout most of Europe

Three-spined Stickleback

This little fish has a slender body with flattened sides. It is brownish green on top, with silvery sides. During the breeding season, males become bright red on the belly and throat. The Three-spined Stickleback gets its name from two long spines on its back, and a third shorter spine just in front of the back fin. In spring and summer, the male builds a nest out of bits of plants. He entices the female to lay her eggs in the nest and then he guards the eggs and young inside. You'll find the Three-spined Stickleback in most types of fresh water, but not stagnant ponds. They feed on crustaceans, worms, insects and other small animals.

Group: Sticklebacks (Gasterosteidae)
Size: Up to about 8 cm long
Distribution: Throughout Europe; not in mountainous regions

Perch

The Perch is one of
the most familiar and colourful
European freshwater fish. It has a slender, olive-
green body and two fins on its back, the first with
sharp spines and a dark spot at the rear. Look for 5
to 8 dark, vertical bars on the sides and the deep
orange colour of the fins on the underside. The
belly is cream. Perch live in large ponds, lakes, slow
rivers and canals. They move around in shoals
feeding mainly on leeches, shrimps, caddis and
midge larvae, and small fish. Females drape their
long white egg ribbons around plants and
submerged branches.

Group: Perch (Percidae)
Size: Very variable; up to about 50 cm long
Distribution: Throughout most of Europe

Wandering Snail

This snail is so common that you should be able to
find it in almost any fresh water. It can survive in
anything from high mountain streams to small
garden ponds. The thin shell is pale to dark
yellowish brown and has one large 'body whorl'
with a very large opening. The other three or four
whorls form a small, short spire. Sometimes the
outside of the shell gets 'furred up' like the inside
of a kettle.

Group: Pond snails
(Limnaeidae)
Shell height: 1.5–2.5 cm
Distribution: Throughout Europe

When it is living in fresh water, the snake-like Eel is
usually dark brown above and yellowish below. It
has a long fin beginning in the middle of its back
and continuing all the way round the tail and on to
the underside. Eels are found in all types of fresh
water that are accessible from the sea. They can
move overland through wet areas. They lurk in the
bottom mud feeding on worms, molluscs
and crustaceans, as well as on dead fish
and waste. When they are ready to
breed, at between about 7 to 19 years
old, the eels journey downstream to
the sea. They turn silvery below and black
above. They swim right across the Atlantic to
the Sargasso Sea where they spawn and then die.
The eggs hatch into leaf-shaped larvae which
drift back to the coasts of Europe. Here, they
change into young eels, called 'elvers', and swim
back up the rivers and streams.

European Eel

Group: Eels (Anguillidae)
Size: Up to about 100 cm long
Distribution: Throughout
coastal Europe

Sponges & Worms

Spotted Flatworm

Like all flatworms, this creature has a thin, flat, soft body. It has a triangular-shaped head and two simple, black eyes. As the name suggests, it has spots and streaks all over its body. Its mouth is on the underside, and it crawls along on muddy bottoms of ponds, lakes, slow rivers, and streams, and feeds on decaying matter there. Flatworms look like blobs of jelly out of water. They will expand and glide around if put in a dish of water.

Group: Flatworms (Turbellaria)
Size: Up to 2 cm – Distribution: Scattered throughout Europe, an introduced species from North America

Freshwater Sponge

A sponge looks more like a plant than an animal. It consists of a spongy mass attached to solid objects such as rocks and sunken logs. Inside the sponge is a network of tiny tunnels through which it draws water containing oxygen and tiny floating animals (plankton) on which it feeds. Freshwater sponges vary in shape and colour. Look on the undersides of rocks for yellowish or greyish crusts. On twigs you may find long finger-like, brownish growths. In clear water where there is good light, these will be green because microscopic (tiny) algae grow in the sponge's cells. Sponges will grow in still or running water, but cannot survive in polluted and very stagnant water. In winter, the sponge's body disintegrates. All that remains are tiny balls the size of pin-heads called 'gemmules'. These grow into new sponges in spring.

Group: Sponges (Porifera)
Size: very variable; fingers up to about 20 cm long
Distribution: Widespread throughout Europe

Flatworm (Dendrocoelum)

Like all flatworms, this creature has a flat, soft body, with a definite head and tiny eyes. When you find them, many look like blobs of jelly. Put in a container of water, they will spread out and glide smoothly over the bottom. This species is easy to identify because it is large and is white or greyish. Its body is very sticky. Most flatworms feed on decaying matter, but this one hunts for prey. It traps water lice in strings of sticky mucus which it secretes. Then it sucks out their insides with its tube-like mouth which is underneath its body.

Group: Flatworms (Platyhelminthes)
Size: Up to 2. 5 cm long
Distribution: Common throughout Europe

Flatworm (Polycelis)

This flatworm is different from other flatworms because it has many tiny eyes. Most other common flatworms have only two. It is usually black or brownish, but can be green, reddish or yellow. They can be found by collecting a netful of debris and leaving it to settle in a container of water. The worms will then often crawl out of the mud.

Group: Flatworms (Platyhelminthes)
Size: Up to about 1. 5 cm long
Distribution: Throughout Europe

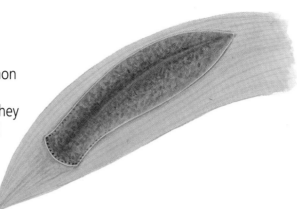

Square-tailed Worm

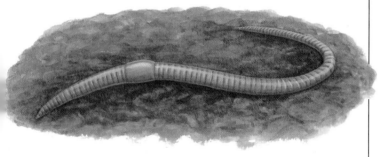

This worm is the only sort of earthworm that can live in water. It is a drab, pinkish-brown in colour, or sometimes reddish or yellowish. It looks just like an earthworm, but the rear half of its body is square in cross section, not round. Look for a smooth patch, called the 'clitellum' or saddle, near the middle of the body. It lives in mud around plant roots or under stones both in the water and on the banks and edges.

Group: Earthworms (Lumbricidae)
Size: Up to about 8 cm long
Distribution: Widespread throughout Europe

Mud or Sludge Worms

These worms are long, thin, and reddish, a colour which comes from the blood. They live in the mud at the bottom of lakes, stagnant ponds, or polluted rivers. They are able to survive in poor conditions because they do not need much oxygen. They build soft mud tubes in which they live head down, with their tails waving about in the water. You may see them in aquarium shops, where they are sold as fish food.

Group: Tubifex Worms (Tubificidae)
Size: Up to 6 cm long
Distribution: Common throughout Europe

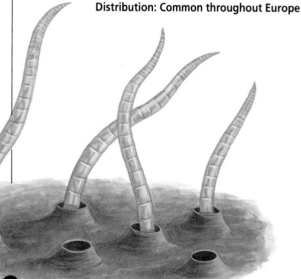

A Collecting Trip

You don't need much equipment, and you certainly don't need to be an expert naturalist to find and study water creatures. Wear old clothes and rubber boots or old trainers, as the area around the pond may be quite muddy. Don't forget to take this field guide! When you get there, don't run or stamp around on the bank, and don't shout. The noise will frighten animals away.

What to take

You may also find the following things useful:

1 **Fishing net** (buy one from a pet shop).
2 **Underwater viewing box** (see right for how to make it).
3 **Empty, white margarine or ice cream container** for watching your catch.
4 **A pipette (eye-dropper) or paintbrush** for moving small animals without hurting them.
5 **Glass or plastic jars with screw-on lids** for carrying species home.
6 **Your field note book, with pens and pencils** for note-taking.
7 **Magnifying glass**. Buy one labelled x4 or x6 and wear it on a string around your neck.
8 **Cmera** to record the various sites you visit.
9 **Lightweight backpack** to carry everything in.

Waterside Safety Code

1 **Always keep your eyes and ears open for danger.** Rivers can be cold and deep.
2 **Always go with an adult** when you go near a river. Stay near your group and stay in sight.
3 **Don't wade into water unless an adult says it is safe to do so.** Never go deeper than rubber boot height.
4 **Don't splash water at other people or push them over in the river.**
5 **Cover any cuts or scratches** with waterproof plasters and rubber gloves before starting work.
6 **Don't get river water in your mouth** or anything that has been in it (including fingers)!

Underwater viewing box

Making your own viewing box for the water will allow you to watch water creatures and their activities in their natural habitat.

1 **Find a plastic container** such as an old bucket or wastepaper basket. Get an adult to cut the bottom out leaving a rim about 3 cm wide.

Handling amphibians

You may be able to catch newts, young salamanders, frogs or toads using a fishing net in a pond (see page 30). Most salamanders, newts and frogs can be safely handled. But remember, amphibians are 'cold-blooded' and have soft, moist skins. They do not like being held in warm, dry hands. Tip them into a plastic tub with some damp vegetation. When you have finished looking at them, put them back where you found them.

Some toads and a few salamanders can secrete an unpleasant liquid from their skins. This can cause swelling and discomfort if it enters a cut or gets in your mouth or eyes. **Rinse the affected part with clean water as soon as possible if this happens.**

Keeping records

Making notes and quick drawings in your field notebook will help you identify fast-moving animals. Transfer your notes into a ring binder when you get home and record each trip on a separate sheet of paper. Stick in your sketches, photos, and any other samples you may have collected during your expedition.

1 **When you visit a new site,** give it a name, write down the date and what sort of habitat it is (pond, river, marsh, etc.).
2 **Each time you visit that site,** record what the weather was like and what time of day it was.
3 **When you see an animal,** watch it carefully. Make a note of its shape, colour and size to help identification.
4 **Write down what the animal was doing** (swimming, eating, resting, etc.), how many there were, and if it was making a noise.

2 **Get an adult to cut a piece of clear perspex or plastic** to fit inside the container.
3 **Stick it down on to the rim** with waterproof adhesive – you can buy this from a pet shop.
4 **Take your viewing box along to a pond,** lake, or reservoir. Find a safe place, carefully lean over the bank and place the clear plastic end of your box in the water. Look through the hole for snails crawling, fish swimming, and other creatures.
5 **You can also wade upstream** in shallow streams and rivers, wearing your rubber boots. These areas are good for finding mussels. A sunny day is best.

Ponds & Lakes

All ponds have still, shallow water. Shallow water means that light can penetrate to the bottom, allowing water weeds to grow. The weeds provide food and shelter for many animals. Because the water is still, there is not very much oxygen in it, and it may be stagnant (not moving and therefore dirty) near the bottom. Only animals that can put up with this can live in ponds.

Many pond snails, and all frogs, toads, newts, and reptiles can live in stagnant water because they come to the surface to breathe. Others, such as tadpoles, have very large gills to help them take enough oxygen from the water.

Most ponds are made by people. Small ponds often have to be looked after to stop sedges, rushes, and other swamp plants from growing right into them and filling them up. Many animals found in ponds and lakes will also be found in slow-moving streams and rivers (see pages 56–63) where conditions are very like a pond. As many natural wetlands are now being destroyed, ponds are becoming more and more important as refuges for water animals. This picture shows twelve animals from this book; see how many you can identify.

Copepod, Daphnia (in circle);
Bitterling, Caddisfly Larva, Dragonfly Nymph,
Frog Spawn, Chinamark Moth Larva, Smooth Newts,
Great Ramshorn Snail, Marsh Spider,
Water Spider, Toad Spawn.

Common Toad

With its large, plump body and very warty, brown or reddish-brown skin, the Common Toad is easy to recognize. It lives in damp places in woods, gardens and fields. At night, toads come out to hunt for insects, worms and slugs, and so are very useful in the garden. The larger females may even catch frogs or mice. During the winter, the Common Toad hibernates in the ground. Then in early spring, toads migrate several kilometres to their favourite pond, usually the one they were born in. There they mate and lay long strings of eggs (see page 25).

Group: Typical Toads (Bufonidae)
Size: Up to 15 cm long
Distribution: Throughout Europe, except Ireland

Natterjack Toad

You can tell this small greenish toad from the Common Toad by the yellow stripe running down its back. The Natterjack lives in sandy areas and among sand dunes at the seaside, making use of temporary ponds that later dry up. It is active by night, and feeds on insects, worms and slugs. It prefers to run rather than walk or hop, and is sometimes called the Running Toad. Look out: do not pick up this toad, as it is a protected species in Great Britain.

Group: Typical Toads (Bufonidae)
Size: Up to 8 cm long
Distribution: From Spain and Portugal, north-east to Denmark and Russia; now rare in Great Britain

Painted Frog

This little frog has shiny skin which may be brownish, yellowish or grey with darker spots. Look closely at the eye which has a triangular pupil – typical frogs have horizontal pupils. It lives in marshes, ponds and flowing water in low-lying land. It feeds on worms, insects and small fish. It catches its prey with its jaws rather than its tongue which is disc-shaped and cannot shoot out very far.

Group: Painted Frogs and Toads (Discoglossidae)
Size: Up to 7 cm long
Distribution: Spain and Portugal, parts of French Pyrenees, Sicily and Malta

Striped-necked Terrapin

This terrapin has an oval, black or brown shell with paler spots and streaks. It is easy to tell from tortoises, which sometimes come near water, because they have much higher domed shells. There is only one other European terrapin, the pond terrapin (see opposite). The Striped-necked Terrapin lives in still or slow-flowing waters where it can catch worms, snails, fish, frogs and newts. It can live to be 70 years old.

Group: Terrapins (Emydidae)
Size: Up to 20 cm long
Distribution: Spain, Portugal and the Balkans

European Pond Terrapin

This terrapin has an oval, black or brown shell with paler spots and streaks. It is easy to tell from tortoises, which sometimes come near the water, because these have much higher domed shells. There is only one other European terrapin, the stripe-necked terrapin, found in Spain, Portugal and the Balkans (see opposite). The Pond Terrapin lives in still or slow-flowing waters where it can catch worms, snails, fish, frogs and newts. It can live to be 70 years old.

Group: Terrapins (Emydidae)
Size: Up to 20 cm long
Distribution: Most of Europe, but not Great Britain or northern Europe

Parsley Frog

This little frog is agile, and can swim, jump and even climb. It is grey or olive with bright parsley-green spots and sometimes orange warts on its sides. The Parsley Frog lives in damp places and around ponds that have lots of plant life. During the day, it hides under stones or in holes in the ground. It comes out at night to find food such as worms and insects. Males make a deep croaking sound underwater, and a weak squeak in the air.

Group: Spadefoot Frogs (Pelobatidae)
Size: Up to 5 cm long
Distribution: western Belgium, France, Spain, Portugal, northwestern Italy

Fire-bellied Toad

It's easy to see how this toad got its name! Its belly has bright red and black marks and white spots. By contrast, its back is dark brown. It lives in still, shallow water such as pools and ponds, and feeds on insects and worms. The Fire-bellied Toad is active by day, when it hides among plants in and by the water. In winter, it hibernates on land. All through the summer breeding season, males croak together, making a noise that sounds like distant rumbling. Be careful not to touch this toad as, if attacked, it releases a nasty liquid that may sting you.

Group: Painted Frogs and Toads (Discoglossidae)
Size: Up to 5 cm long
Distribution: Eastern Europe only, from Denmark, eastwards to the Balkans

Midwife Toad

This little brown toad hides under stones or in holes during the day, and comes out at night. It gets its name from the unusual behaviour of the males. Several males compete for a female. The male that wins the female mates with her and then drapes her eggs in a string around his own hind legs. He carries the eggs everywhere he goes, making sure they always have enough moisture and do not get damaged. Eventually, he takes them to a pond to hatch (see page 25).

Group: Painted Frogs and Toads (Discoglossidae)
Size: Up to 5 cm long
Distribution: Western Europe, including Spain, France and Germany

Yellow-bellied Toad

This little toad looks dull at first sight with its grey, brown or olive warty back. If frightened, it turns over and reveals a brilliant yellow and black belly which scares off its enemies. The Yellow-bellied Toad lives in ponds, ditches and forest pools and puddles in both lowland and mountainous areas. It is active by day and can be seen in large groups spread-eagled on the water surface. It hibernates on land in the winter. Be careful not to touch this toad as, if attacked, it releases a nasty liquid that may sting you.

Group: Painted Frogs and Toads (Discoglossidae)
Size: Up to 5 cm long
Distribution: Most of central Europe south of Great Britain, not Spain and Portugal

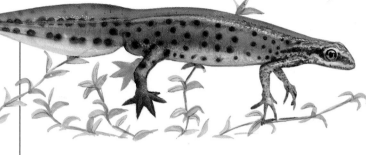

Marbled Newt

This is the only green European newt. It has black marbling on top, and a grey belly. Males and females look similar except during the breeding season in the spring. Then, the male develops a crest along his back with vertical stripes. Most females and young have an orange stripe along the middle of the back. During breeding time, Marbled Newts live in springs, slow-flowing streams and pools in low-lying areas. For the rest of the time, they live mostly on dry ground. They feed on worms, snails and insect larvae.

Group: Salamanders & Newts (Salamandridae)
Size: Up to 14 cm long
Distribution: Spain, Portugal
and southwestern France

Palmate Newt

This small, smooth-skinned newt is brownish-olive with small dark spots. Its belly is a paler yellow than that of the smooth newt and it has an unspotted throat. Look too for a dark stripe running through each eye. In the breeding season, males have a thin filament sticking out of their tail. They also develop a low, smooth crest on the back and tail. Look for them in ponds and shallow water from March onwards. They spend the winter on land.

Group: Salamanders & Newts
(Salamandridae)
Size: Up to 9 cm
Distribution: From northern Spain,
through France, Germany and
Great Britain; not Ireland

Sharp-ribbed Salamander

This creature is one of the largest amphibians that you can see in Europe. The name 'sharp-ribbed' comes from the row of bright orange bumps along its sides, under which are the rib tips. The body is greyish, and covered with black spots. This salamander lives in ponds, ditches, lakes, marshes and slow-flowing water. It is mainly active at night, when it ventures out and goes in search of food. This food consists of wireworms and earthworms.

Group: Salamanders & Newts (Salamandridae)
Size: About 20 cm long; can reach 30 cm
Distribution: Spain and Portugal

Smooth Newt

It is easy to confuse this newt with the Palmate Newt as it is a very similar colour. However its belly is usually orange, rather than yellow, and has more spots. It also has a spotted throat and five faint stripes along the head. In the breeding season, males are easy to identify. They develop a tall, wavy crest all along the back and tail which is not so spiky as on the Crested Newt. Look for the Smooth Newt in early spring in weedy ponds and ditches. After breeding they can be found under damp logs, piles of stones and in crevices on land.

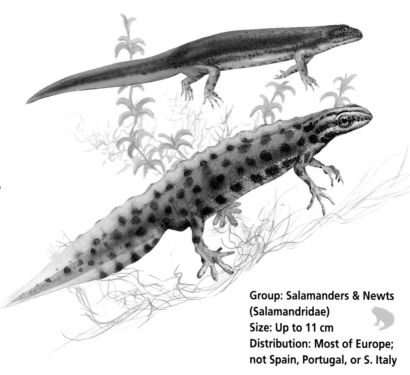

Group: Salamanders & Newts (Salamandridae)
Size: Up to 11 cm
Distribution: Most of Europe; not Spain, Portugal, or S. Italy

Crested Newt

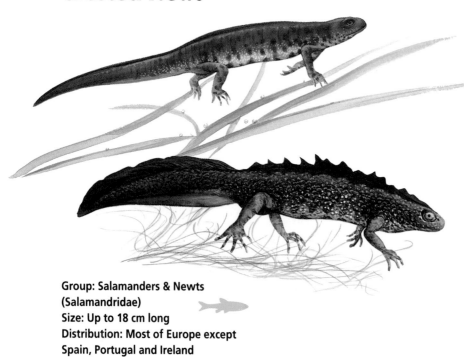

Group: Salamanders & Newts (Salamandridae)
Size: Up to 18 cm long
Distribution: Most of Europe except Spain, Portugal and Ireland

This is the largest European newt – it is also known as the Warty Newt, because of its warty skin, which is dark grey or brown with large black spots. Its belly is orange with black spots. In the breeding season the male is easy to identify. He develops a big, toothed crest on his back and another one on his tail. The female has no crest on her back, and only a narrow border around her tail. The Crested Newt lives in still or slow-flowing water, and feeds on worms, snails, and insect larvae. When on land, it can be seen only at night or in damp weather. Look out: do not pick up this newt, as it is a protected species in Great Britain.

Newt Spawn & Tadpoles

Female newts lay their eggs singly, and carefully wrap each one in the leaf of a water plant for protection. When the larvae hatch out, they are pale and almost transparent, and look rather like frog tadpoles. But soon they grow feathery gills on each side of the neck. Over a few months, they gradually become like adult newts. The front legs grow first, then the hind legs. Often, young newts spend their first winter in the mud at the bottom of the pond.

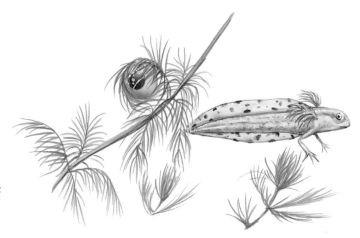

Frog Spawn & Tadpoles

In the spring, female frogs lay their eggs in a mass. Each egg looks like a black dot surrounded by a protective jelly. Floating masses of the eggs of the Common Frog are quite a familiar sight in ponds. Other frogs may lay their eggs in weed beneath the water surface. The eggs hatch into tadpoles. At first, they look like black commas. Then gradually they grow gills, tails, hind legs and lastly front legs. Frog tadpoles are a dark greeny-brown. Eventually, the tail and the gills are absorbed, and little frogs hop out of the pond.

Toad Spawn & Tadpoles

Toads lay their eggs in long, jelly-like strings. Some, like the Common Toad, have a double row of eggs. Others, like the Natterjack Toad, have only a single row. These strings become tangled around stems of plants. They hatch into tadpoles that look almost identical to those of frogs, but toad tadpoles tend to be smaller and darker than frog tadpoles. They also develop in a very similar way. The hind legs grow first, then the front legs. Then the tail is absorbed, and the toads leave the water.

Pike

Group: Pikes (Esocidae)
Size: Up to 130 cm
Distribution: Most of Europe

This big fish is easy to recognize, with its long body and duckbill-shaped snout. Its jaws are lined with sharp, pointed teeth, with which it kills and eats many fish, as well as frogs, insects, mice and even birds. Its body is greenish, with white or yellow spots. It swims in cold-water lakes, reservoirs and weed-choked rivers. Left undisturbed, it can live as long as twenty-four years.

Tench

This fish is easy to identify with its stocky, rounded body, fat tail and rounded fins. If you touch one, it will feel very slimy and smooth. Its colour is greenish brown with bronze sides and a creamy-brown belly. There is also an attractive golden form often kept in ornamental ponds. It has a long, fleshy growth known as a 'barbel' on either side of its mouth, which it uses to feel along the bottom mud of lakes and pools where it lives. Tench can survive in very muddy and stagnant ponds. Its food consists of crustaceans, water insects, molluscs and water plants.

Group: Carps and Minnows (Cyprinidae)
Size: Up to 70 cm long; usually 30–50 cm long
Distribution: Widespread throughout Europe

Belica

Also known as the Sunbleak, this slender fish is a brilliant silver colour, with an olive back and a silvery blue strip along its sides. It has quite a big head, with no scales on it. Its body has scales which come off easily. The Belica is a sociable fish and many of them live together in 'schools', in still waters and slow-flowing rivers. It prefers waters with a lot of plant life, and feeds on small animals, often coming to the surface to take insects.

Group: Carps and Minnows (Cyprinidae)
Size: Up to 12 cm long
Distribution: Throughout mainland Europe, but not Great Britain

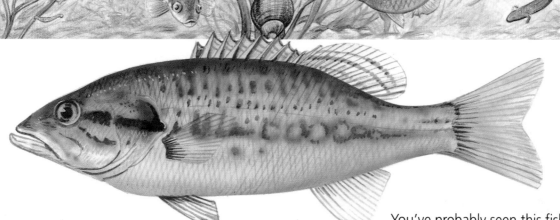

Large-mouth Bass

This fish has a slender body with flattened sides, a big head, and, as the name suggests, a big mouth. It is dark olive above and white below, with a broad, broken stripe along its sides. It has two fins on its back. The first fin has ten stiff spines, the second has one spine and soft rays. You'll find this fish in slow rivers and lakes, where it feeds on other fish. This species has been introduced from North America.

Group: Black basses (Centrarchidae)
Size: Up to 83 cm long, usually less
Distribution: Western Europe, including southern England

Goldfish

You've probably seen this fish more in fish bowls than in the wild, but it lives in the warmer waters of Europe. As its name suggests, the Goldfish is a goldish orange colour, with scales that are easy to see. It has a long back fin which has one serrated spine. This fish likes warm water that has plenty of plants in it, where it feeds on water insects, molluscs and crustaceans as well as plants.

Group: Carps and Minnows (Cyprinidae)
Size: Up to 40 cm
Distribution: Southern Europe

American Bullhead

This is a type of catfish, so it has dark whiskers called 'barbels' on its chin. It is a mottled chocolate-brown color with a yellowish or milk-white belly. As with all catfish, there is a small, rayless fin between its back and tail fins. The Bullhead lives in muddy-bottomed ponds and lakes, and in slow streams and rivers. It uses its barbels to feel along the bottom muck for the insect larvae and molluscs that it eats. The female lays eggs in a scoop in the mud, which the male guards carefully.

Group: Catfishes (Ictaluridae)
Size: Up to 50 cm
Distribution: Introduced to Europe. Not Britain

Common Carp

This Carp can be recognized by its fat body, its scales which give a crisscross pattern, and its long back fin. At the front of this fin is a hard, serrated ray, but the rest of the rays are soft. The Carp is a golden-olive colour and has two short barbels on each side of its jaw. It prefers to live in warm water and can be seen in quiet ponds, lakes, and sluggish rivers which have plants in them. Favourite foods include molluscs, crustaceans and insect larvae, as well as algae and plants. Females lay eggs in the spring, which stick to plants, or sink to the bottom.

Group: Carps and Minnows (Cyprinidae)
Size: Up to 75 cm long
Distribution: Found throughout Europe

The **Mirror Carp** is a variety of the Common Carp that has been especially bred in captivity. It is silvery in colour with a single row of very large, plate-like scales along the sides of its body. These give it its name. Mirror Carp are found both in ornamental ponds and lakes and in the wild. Many other forms of domesticated carp have been bred, including the very valuable, multi-coloured, 'Koi' Carp. White, orange, red, blue and black varieties also exist.

The **Leather Carp** is another domesticated variety of the Common Carp which can be found both in captivity and in the wild. It has no scales at all and feels very smooth to the touch.

Nine-spined Stickleback

This fish is slender, and, as its name suggests, has a row of spines on its back. It doesn't always have exactly nine spines – there can be any number between seven and twelve. The colour is dull brown and blotchy above, and silvery on the belly. It may live in fresh or salt water, as long as it is cold. It prefers densely weeded, shallow waters such as small ponds and streams.

Group: Sticklebacks (Gasterosteidae)
Size: Up to 5 cm long

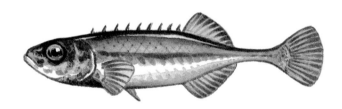

Distribution: Cold waters of northern, central and eastern Europe

Pumpkinseed

This fish is also called the Common Sunfish. It has a fat body, which is tan or pale yellow, and its sides are covered in spots. There is also a scattering of tiny brown spots on the tail fin. A good identification guide is the brightly coloured gill cover which has a black and orange tip. The back fin has stiff spines. You'll find them swimming in streams, ponds, and lakes with plenty of plants in them. It feeds on molluscs, insects, and fish. In the summer, males scoop out saucer-shaped nests in the bottom sand or gravel. Then females lay their eggs in them.

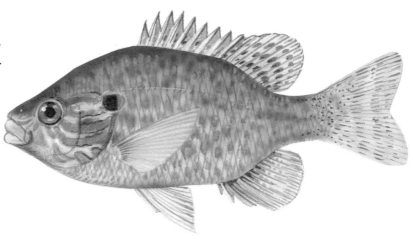

Group: Sunfishes (Centrarchidae)
Size: Up to 25 cm long
Distribution: Introduced to warmer parts of Europe

Bitterling

This little fish is thin, but tall and is covered with large scales. It has one high fin on its back and a forked tail fin. Its head is small, with large eyes. The colour varies at different seasons, but is typically grey-brown on top, with silvery sides which have a pink flush. There is also a shiny blue-green stripe near its tail. The Bitterling lives in small ponds, lakes and slow-flowing rivers, and feeds on crustaceans in the plankton, and water insect larvae. It has a rather unusual breeding pattern. Females lay their eggs inside freshwater mussesl (see pages 63 and 72), and two to three weeks later, the young fish swim out of their shelly birthplace.

Group: Carps and Minnows (Cyprinidae)
Size: Up to 7 cm long
Distribution: Central Europe and the Danube basin; introduced to western Europe, including Great Britain

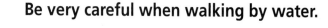

Explore a Pond

Exploring a pond is an easy way to find out more about freshwater life. Ponds are often teeming with little creatures, and the area around a pond is home to many others. Always take a friend and always tell an adult when you go exploring.

Be very careful when walking by water.

Pond dipping

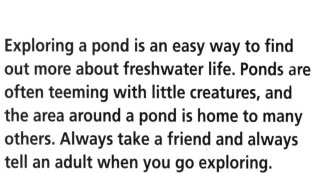

Pond dipping is exactly what it sounds like: it involves dipping a net into a pond and seeing what you come up with. Spring is probably the best time to go pond dipping. Then, there is not too much weed, and there are lots of adult beetles, bugs, tadpoles, and newts.

If you want to see insect larvae such as dragonfly nymphs, go in the summer. They hatch in the spring, and by the summer they will have grown to their full size. Winter is best for creatures like the shrimps that live in temporary ponds. These types of ponds form in the autumn and dry up in spring.

1 **You will need a simple net with a mesh of about 2 mm**. If the mesh is too fine it will clog up. If it is too big, it won't catch anything small.
2 **Approach the water's edge quietly**. Any sudden noise or movement will send the pond creatures running for cover.
3 **Sweep your net across the surface of the pond** for surface-dwelling insects like beetles, pond skaters, water boatmen, and water mites.
4 **Scoop the net gently under pond weeds,** brushing the weed to knock off animals living and crawling on it such as tadpoles, damselfly nymphs, mayfly nymphs or snails.
5 **Gently push the net along the surface of the bottom mud**. Be careful not to scoop too deep or it will fill up with muck. Here, you may find flatworms, caddisfly cases, worms and shrimps.
6 **Put your finds into your container** with water from the pond.
7 **When you have finished examining them**, return them gently to the water.

Be careful which animals you put together: newts, beetle larvae, and dragonfly nymphs will eat other creatures such as tadpoles.

Examining very small animals

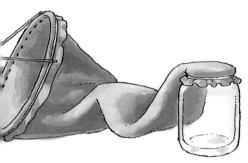

1 **Make a tapering net with a very fine mesh,** like muslin or an old nylon curtain.
2 **Cut a hole in the end of the net** and tie the end around the mouth of a plastic jam jar.
3 **Walk round the pond trailing the net with its jar.** Keep it in the clear water above the bottom and away from weeds. Keep going for some minutes. The animals you catch will be washed down into the jar and will collect there.

4 **Lift the jar up and look at it.** It should be full of tiny moving specks, such as water fleas, and copepods. Use your magnifying glass to examine your catch.

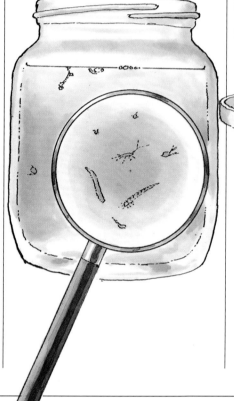

5 **If you have a microscope,** you can use it to look at your catch more closely. Use an eye dropper or a baby's medicine dropper to transfer drops of water to a small shallow dish such as a jar lid. You will see them better if they can't move too far.
6 **Experiment with different coloured backgrounds** and lights to see how best to show up the animals.

Mud grubbing

The mud at the bottom of a pond is a good place to look for worms and other animals that can put up with low oxygen levels and not much light.

The best way to find these is to scoop up some mud and debris with your net or a bucket and sieve it, a little at a time (use an old kitchen sieve). Hold the sieve half in the water and shake it gently The mud floats away leaving the animals behind.

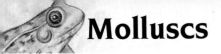

Molluscs

Great Pond Snail

This snail has a tan-coloured, almost transparent shell, with a sharp spire on the top. The first whorl is large, up to half the total height. It is also called the Stagnant Pond Snail as it can survive in stagnant waters. This is because it breathes air, and comes to the water surface at regular intervals. It can be found in large ponds and lakes, as well as in ditches and marshes. The Great Pond Snail is the biggest pond snail of all.

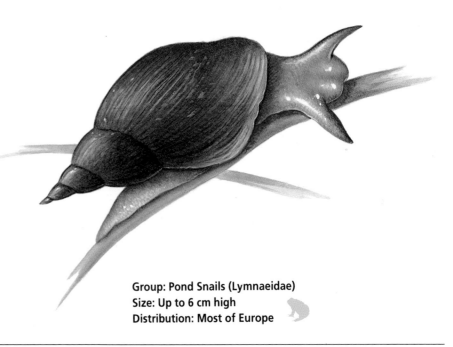

Group: Pond Snails (Lymnaeidae)
Size: Up to 6 cm high
Distribution: Most of Europe

Zebra Mussel

This pretty mussel is named for its zebra-like, zig-zag stripes, which may become worn away with time. It attaches itself to firm surfaces such as rocks or underwater branches by a bunch of sticky threads known as the 'byssus'. It may form great colonies in canals, lakes and reservoirs. Like other mussels, it feeds by sucking in water through a tube-shaped siphon, filtering out food and then ejecting the waste water through another siphon. This species originated in eastern Europe, but has spread widely over the last two centuries.

Group: Freshwater Mussels (Dreissenidae)
Size: Up to 4 cm long
Distribution: Most of Europe

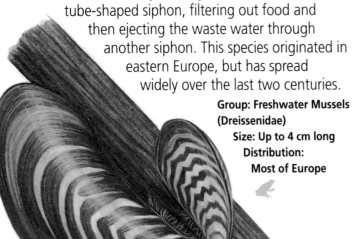

Great Ramshorn Snail

This snail has a very large shell which is reddish brown to olive and has a glossy texture. The shell does not come to a point, but forms a flat coil with five to six whorls. It looks like a ram's horn, hence the snail's name. The animal inside the shell is deep reddish brown in colour. The Great Ramshorn Snail lives in ponds, lakes and sluggish rivers. Search for it under lily leaves and other plants.

Group: Ramshorn Snails (Planorbidae)
Size: Up to 3 cm across
Distribution: Most of Europe, but not the far north or south

Moss Bladder Snail

This snail has a fragile, slender shell which tapers to a point. It is a smooth, shiny brownish colour, and is almost transparent. The shell opening is narrow and oval. The animal itself is almost black. Moss Bladder Snails live in temporary ponds and ditches that may dry up in the summer.

Group: Bladder Snails (Physidae)
Size: Up to 1.5 cm high – Distribution: Most of Europe

Common Ramshorn Snail

This snail looks rather like the Great Ramshorn, only much smaller. The pale to dark brown shell forms a flat coil of five to six whorls. There are many different kinds of Ramshorn Snails which are difficult to tell apart, but the group is easy to recognize. The Ramshorn Snail lives in marshes, ponds, lakes and rivers, particularly where the water is shallow and there are a lot of weeds growing.

Group: Ramshorn Snails (Planorbidae)
Size: Up to 1.5 cm across
Distribution: Most of Europe

Lake Limpet

You will have to search hard to find this little limpet. It lives in a similar way to seaside limpets, but is much smaller. You will find it clamped on to plants or stones in clean still waters. It has a narrow, low shell and the top is curved backwards and off to one side.

Group: Lake Limpets (Acroloxidae)
Size: Up to 7 mm long; 2 mm high
Distribution: Throughout Europe

Ear Snail

This snail's shell has a huge opening in proportion to the rest of it. It is spiral in shape, with a short, narrow cone at the top, and is light greenish brown to yellowish brown. The last whorl before the opening has an earlike flare, which gives it its name. You'll find the Ear Snail in lakes, ponds, and slow-flowing streams among lily pads and reeds.

Group: Pond Snails (Lymnaeidae)
Size: Up to 3 cm high
Distribution: Most of Europe

Tadpole Shrimp

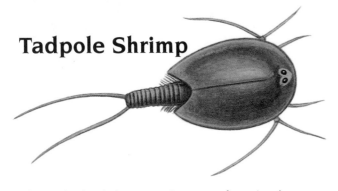

The Tadpole Shrimp gets its name from its shape. It has an oval, shield-like front end and a long thin hind end with two thread-like tails. Like Fairy shrimps, they swim gracefully but upside down! They also creep over the bottom of the temporary pools and ponds in which they live. Here they search for tiny animals to eat or they feed on dead tadpoles and frogs' eggs.

Group: Crustaceans
Size: Up to 10 cm including tail
Distribution: Throughout Europe. Rare in Great Britain.

Seed Shrimp

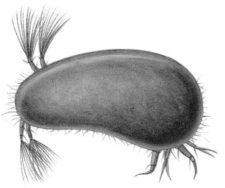

!f you see tiny seeds with legs crawling about in your net, you have caught some seed shrimps! These common animals have two shells joined by a hinge and look rather like minute, hairy sea shells. They crawl about feeding on decaying plants in quiet, shallow water. With a fine net, you may catch white, yellow, grey, red, brown or green ones.

Group: Ostracods (Crustaceans)
Size: 0.5 to 5 mm
Distribution: Throughout Europe

Opossum Shrimp

Most shrimps and prawns live in the sea, but the delicate Opossum Shrimp is found in deep lakes and sometimes in rivers. It has an almost transparent, humped body, and swims with eight pairs of feathery legs. It is called the Opossum Shrimp because the female carries her eggs and young around In a special pouch. An opossum is a furry, rat-like animal with a pouch like a kangaroo.

Group: Mysid crustaceans
Size: Up to 2 cm long
Distribution: Northern Europe

Fairy Shrimps

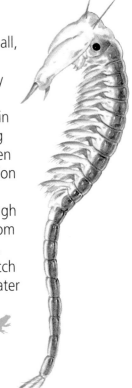

These little creatures live in small, temporary pools often in woodlands or old forests. They appear miraculously in spring when snow and ice melt or rain fills potholes. They swim along upside-down, using their eleven pairs of leaflike legs. This motion also brings them food in the water to filter. Females lay tough eggs which sink into the bottom mud. When the pool dries up, the eggs survive there and hatch out when a fresh supply of water fills the pool.

Group: Fairy Shrimps (Anostraca)
Size: Up to 4.5 cm long
Distribution: Found throughout Europe

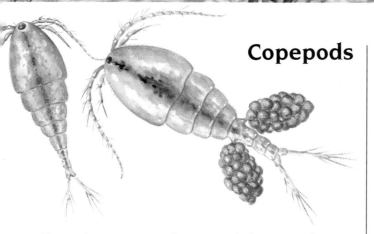

Copepods

These tiny creatures often occur in huge numbers. They live in any kind of still, freshwater habitat, from ponds to puddles. They use their legs or their antennae to swim along. Females have egg sacs which hang on either side of the body. They are an important food source for other freshwater animals.

Group: Copepods (Copepoda)
Size: Less than 6 mm long
Distribution: Found throughout Europe

Water Fleas

These tiny crustaceans have their whole body enclosed in a thick shell, leaving only the forked antennae free, which are used for swimming. They get their name from their jerky movement. Water Fleas vary in colour, from greenish to brown or red. They can be found in great numbers, in many freshwater habitats, especially ponds. You will need a hand lens to see them clearly.

Group: Water Fleas (Cladocera)
Size: Less than 6 mm long
Distribution: Found throughout Europe

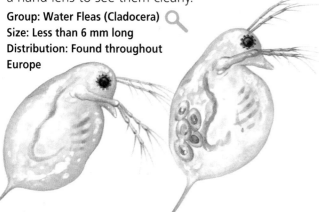

Fish Louse

This creature looks very different to the Water Louse. It has a flat body, a pair of suckers, and four pairs of legs. The Fish Louse is a parasite, which means that it lives off another creature. It clamps its suckers on to a fish's body or fins, and sucks up the blood. It is also a good swimmer, kicking along in the water with its legs. Look closely at the gills and skin of a pike or other freshly caught fish, and you may spot one.

Group: Fish Lice (Branchiura) – Size: Up to 1.5 cm long
Distribution: Found throughout Europe

Water Louse

This creature is a flattened version of the familiar land wood louse. The Water Louse can be found in almost all kinds of water, including puddles. It feeds on decaying plant and animal material. It is unable to swim, but crawls instead over mud and plants. In spring, some ponds teem with thousands of these little animals.

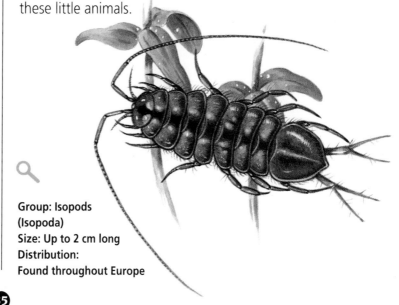

Group: Isopods (Isopoda)
Size: Up to 2 cm long
Distribution: Found throughout Europe

Water Spider

This is the only European spider that lives underwater. It is large and brownish in colour. It lives in a silken domed nest filled with air. This air is carried from the water surface to the nest as a glistening bubble on the spider's hairy abdomen. Males and females usually live in separate nests, and the eggs are laid in the female's nest. Water Spiders hunt for their food, preying on many small water animals.

Group: Spiders (Arachnida)
Size: Up to 1.5 cm long
Distribution: Most of Europe

Raft Spider

Also called the Marsh or Swamp Spider, this large spider is deep brown, with a bright yellow or white band along each side. Unlike the water spider, it spends most of its time on the surface among plants. If alarmed, it will crawl or dive down underwater until the danger passes. It gets its name because it lurks on floating leaves.

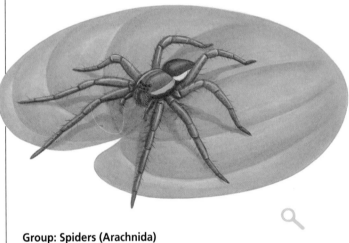

Group: Spiders (Arachnida)
Size: Body up to 2 cm long – Distribution: Most of Europe

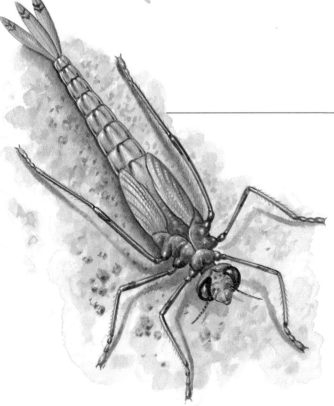

Damselfly Nymph

The adult Damselfly is like a small, slender version of the Dragonfly. Its nymph or young is also more slender than that of the dragonfly. It can easily be identified by the three leaf-like gills at its tail end. It cannot jet propel itself like the Dragonfly Nymph, but it hunts in a similar way, crawling about among the mud and weeds. Look for the empty shells of dragonfly and damselfly nymphs clinging to plants above the water's surface. These are left behind when the nymphs turn into flying adults.

Group: Damselflies (Zygoptera)
Size: Up to 4 cm long
Distribution: Found throughout Europe

Dragonfly Nymph

The whirring wings and bright colours of adult dragonflies are a familiar sight around ponds and lakes. However, these beautiful insects start life as grotesque-looking, brown nymphs which live in the water. They are ferocious hunters with hinged jaws called a mask. When a tadpole or young fish is spotted, the nymph shoots out its mask and seizes the prey. It can swim by jet propulsion, sucking in and squirting water out from the end of its body.

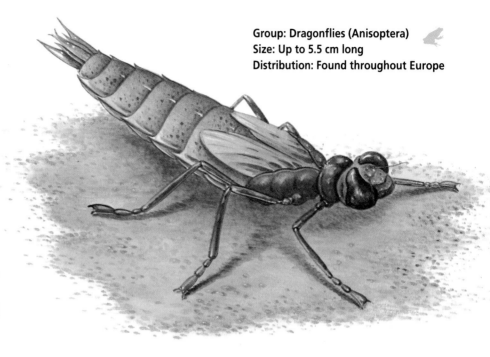

Group: Dragonflies (Anisoptera)
Size: Up to 5.5 cm long
Distribution: Found throughout Europe

Alderfly Larva

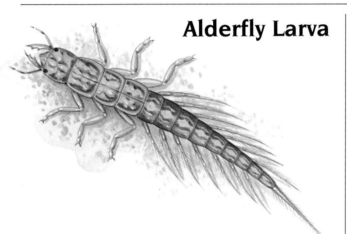

Adult Alderflies can be found hiding among plants by the water's edge. The young Alderfly, or larva, lives in the water at the muddy bottom of ponds, ditches, and streams. It has a long, brown body, with three pairs of legs and seven pairs of thin gills sticking out from it. The tail ends in a single hairy point. It is a hunter and catches its prey with strong pincer-like jaws.

Group: Alderflies (Megaloptera)
Size: Up to 2.5 cm – Distribution: Found throughout Europe

Water Mites

These little creatures are related to the spiders , but are much smaller. Like spiders, they have eight legs. There are many types of water mites , but some may be hard to see as they are so small. Look for them in ponds amongst plant debris or floating on the water surface. The large red ones show up best. Water Mites hunt tiny animals such as water fleas (see opposite), which they seize in their jaws and suck dry using their tube-shaped mouth parts. The larvae of water mites only have six legs and big jaws, which they use to attach themselves to other animals and suck their blood. After a time, they drop off, and eventually change into adult form.

Group: Mites (Acari)
Size: Up to 7 mm, often 0.5–2 mm long
Distribution: Throughout Europe

Insect Larvae (Young)

Phantom Midge Larva

The larvae of the Phantom Midge are transparent, hence the name. The only visible bits are the black eyes and air sacs at the front and back of their bodies, which help them to float horizontally in the middle of the water, and to swim jerkily. Unlike other midge larvae, these are hunters, and use their fang-like mouths to grasp prey such as water fleas.

Group: Non-biting Midges (Chaoborinidae)
Size: Up to 4 mm long
Distribution: Throughout Europe

Screech Beetle Larva

The adult Screech Beetle get its name because of the rasping squeak it makes if removed from the water. However, its larva does not make a sound. It is very striking with its broad head and its black and gold colouring. Look for its three long tails which will help you to recognize it. The larva burrows through mud at the bottom of ponds, searching for worms to feed on.

Group: Screech Beetles (Hygrobiidae)
Size: Up to 12 mm long
Distribution: Across most of Europe

Mosquito Larva

Tiny, wriggling, worm-like mosquito larvae are a familiar sight in water butts, gutters, and any stagnant water. Look at them through a magnifying glass and you will see that each one has a bulbous head and breathes through a tube in its tail, which it sticks out of the water's surface. You will also find them hanging upside-down at the surface of water in small ponds, ditches, bogs, and marshes. Luckily they are a favourite fish food, which helps to keep their numbers down.

Group: Mosquitoes & Gnats (Culicidae)
Size: Up to 12 mm
Distribution: Throughout Europe

Whirligig Beetle Larva

The young of the Whirligig Beetle looks rather like a centipede. However, it has only three pairs of real legs. The rest of its 'legs' are gills (for breathing) along the sides of its body. It hunts along the bottom of ponds and streams for other insect larvae and plants to eat. You can tell this larva from the similar alderfly larva (see page 37) because it does not have a pointed, hairy tail.

Group: Whirligig Beetles (Gyrinidae)
Size: up to 2 cm
Distribution:
Throughout Europe

Diving Beetle Larva

The adult Diving Beetle lives in the water and is a ferocious predator, but its larva is even worse! It can walk along the bottom mud, or swim, using its legs as oars. It will attack anything with its fierce, pincerlike jaws, from tadpoles and insects to fish. It sticks its tail out of the water to take in air through special tubes. Watch out, as it can also give you a nasty nip.

Group: Diving beetles (Dytiscidae)
Size: Up to 7.5 cm
Distribution: Throughout Europe

Crane Fly Larva

Crane Flies, which are popularly known as Daddy-long-legs, have fat, maggot-like larvae which live among mud and stones, in the water. There are many different kinds and some larvae live on land in damp places. They can either come to the surface for air to breathe, or breathe through gills at the tip of their abdomens. They are carnivorous and feed mainly on sludge worms (see page 15).

Group: Crane Flies (Tipulidae)
Size: Up to 3 cm long – Distribution: Throughout Europe

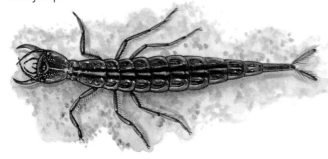

Midge Larva

Midge Larva are also known as Blood Worms because many of them are blood-red. They have segmented, worm-like bodies, with a definite head and small 'false legs' on the tail. They range in size greatly, and many of them live in tubes made of mud and mucus. They may also build cases out of plants or sand, and sometimes swim freely in a looping motion. Look for them in rain butts, water troughs and ponds.

Group: Non-biting Midges (Chironomidae)
Size: Up to 2 cm long – Distribution: Throughout Europe

Rat-tailed Maggot

This strange-looking creature is the larva of a hover fly, the adult of which mimics bees. It has a brownish, slug-like body, with a telescopic breathing tube reaching from its rear end to take in air from the water surface. In this way, it can survive in poor conditions, such as temporary pools and tree holes. The larva eventually pupates and the pupa floats at the water surface until the adult emerges.

Group: Hover Flies (Syrphidae)
Size: Body up to 2 cm, tube up to 3 cm long
Distribution: Great Britain and most of Europe

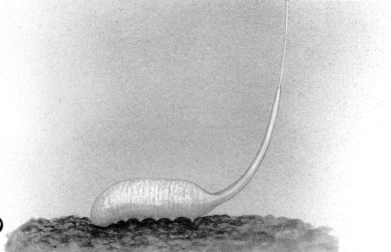

Northern Caddisfly Larva

If you ever see a bundle of twigs walking across the bottom of your collecting bucket, it is probably a Caddisfly Larva. The young of the Caddisfly looks like a caterpillar, if you can ever see it properly. The larva builds a special case to protect itself. The species shown will use anything available to make its case, from tiny sticks arranged in a criss-cross pattern to snail shells and stones, all stuck together. Look out for cases on the bottom while pond-dipping.

Group: Caddis & Sedgeflies (Tricoptera)
Size: Up to 2.5 cm long
Distribution: Throughout Europe

Aquatic Caterpillar (Cataclysta)

This small caterpillar is found among floating masses of duckweed. It is very dark brown, and lives just below the water's surface in a tube made from unevenly shaped pieces of duckweed. It also feeds on duckweed, and makes its case bigger as it grows.
Group: Aquatic Moths (Lepidoptera)
Size: Up to 2 cm long
Distribution: Great Britain and most of Europe

Great Red Sedgefly Larva

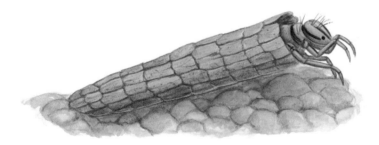

The larva of the Great Red Sedgefly makes a home for itself out of leaf fragments, cut into brick shapes and arranged in a spiral. The case is straight and open at both ends. It carries its case around as it pokes its head and front legs out to prey on insect larvae and crustaceans.
Group: Caddis & Sedgeflies (Tricoptera)
Size: Case is 30–50 mm long
Distribution: Britain & most of Europe

Molanna Caddisfly Larva

This type of Caddisfly Larva builds a different kind of case for its protection. It makes a neat tube, built out of sand, that itself sits on a sandy flat platform. It can be found on sandy bottoms of lakes or ponds, or slow-flowing streams.

Group: Caddis & Sedgeflies (Tricoptera)
Size: Up to 2.5 cm long
Distribution: Throughout Europe

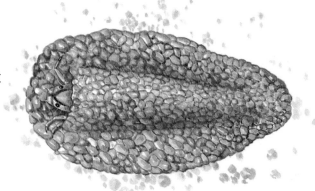

Silverhorn Caddisfly Larva

The larva of the Silverhorn Caddisfly makes its case out of a special secretion. It is a slender, tapering tube, and very lightweight, which allows the larva to swim using its long, paddle-like legs.

Group: Caddis & Sedgeflies (Tricoptera)
Size: Up to 3 cm long, only 3 mm wide
Distribution: Great Britain and most of Europe

Brown China-mark Moth Caterpillar

A few moths have caterpillars that live underwater. The Brown China-mark Moth Caterpillar is brownish in colour and hatches from eggs laid on the underside of floating leaves. It makes a flattish case from two oval pieces of leaf, cut from a water plant and stuck together with silk. It feeds on pondweed, frogbit and water lilies.

Group: Aquatic Moths (Lepidoptera)
Size: Up to 2.5 cm long
Distribution: Great Britain and most of Europe

Green Hydra

This creature has an elastic body which it attaches to a plant. Long, waving tentacles have special stinging cells on them. These paralyze prey such as water fleas, which can then be drawn into the mouth and digested. The Green Hydra looks very like a plant because of its colour. This comes from tiny algae within its body. It lives in clean waters such as spring ponds, duck ponds and ditches. Some ways of finding them are described on page 65. Hydras usually stay attached in one place, like a plant, but they may let go and drift off, or turn somersaults to move along their plant.

Group: Hydroids (Hydrozoa)
Size: Up to 1.5 cm long
Distribution:
Throughout Europe

Leech (Helobdella)

This leech has a ribby, flattened, leaf-shaped body that is very soft. It is pale grey, with a green, yellow, or brownish tinge. There is a tiny, hard scale on its back, but you will need to look very closely to see this! It lives in slow-moving rivers, lakes, and ponds, and feeds by sucking the body fluids of snails.

Group: Leeches (Hirudinea)
Size: 7–30 mm long
Distribution:
Throughout Europe

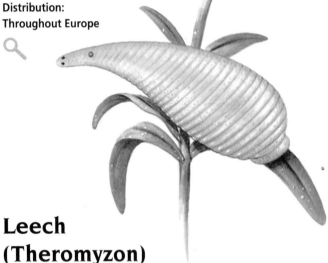

Brown Hydra

This animal is bigger than the Green Hydra, and its tentacles can stretch out up to four or five times the length of its body. It has similar lifestyle and habits to the Green Hydra. Sometimes you may see young Hydras growing out from the adult Hydra. These eventually break off and become independent.

Group: Hydroids (Hydrozoa)
Size: Body up to 3 cm long
Distribution: Throughout Europe

Leech (Theromyzon)

This leech has a soft, almost jellylike, flattened body. It is amber or grey in colour, and large ones have rows of yellow stripes along the back. The underside is pale grey. It feeds by getting into the nasal passages and mouths of water birds, especially ducks, and sucking their blood. When satisfied with its feed, it blows up in size, and may take weeks to digest its meal. It does not swim.

Group: Leeches (Hirudinea)
Size: 12–30 mm
Distribution: Throughout Europe

Fish Leech (Hemiclepsis)

This little leech is quite common in ponds. You can often find one by collecting leaves and debris from the bottom of a pond and spreading it out in a dish. They are easy to spot as they move actively around. Most are a pretty green or brown colour often with yellow spots. It feeds by sucking blood from fish and amphibians such as frogs.

Group: Leeches (Hirudinea)
Size: Up to 2 cm
Distribution: Throughout Europe

Medicinal Leech

This impressive leech is dark greenish with tapestry-like markings of red, yellow and black. It sucks the blood of mammals, including humans, by first piercing the skin with its jaws. It then uses a special compound to let the blood flow freely. It is called 'medicinal' because it used to be collected for medical purposes in the late nineteenth century.

Group: Leeches (Hirudinea)
Size: Up to 11 cm long
Distribution: Most European countries, but now rare

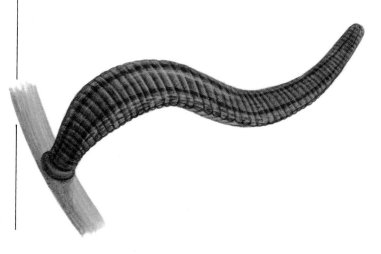

Horse Leech

Group: Leeches (Hirudinea)
Size: Up to 6 cms long (at rest)
Distribution: Throughout Europe

This large leech lives in ponds or marshes, or wanders about in damp places searching for food. It has a stout, flattened body that is yellowish green on top and paler on the underside. The name is misleading because it rarely sucks blood from horses or other large animals. More often, it eats small animals such as earthworms or even small frogs. It swallows them whole, as it has weak jaws with few teeth.

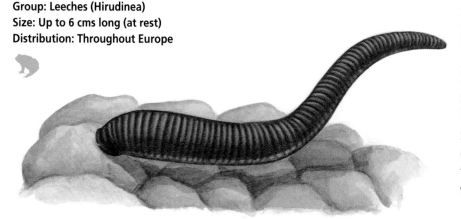

Keeping Tadpoles

Frogs and toads lay their eggs in ponds and streams or other wet places, mostly in spring or summer. Each egg is covered with a thick layer of jelly.

Frogs lay their eggs in large masses which are easy to spot. Most toads produce long strings of eggs and wind them around water plants. Newts and salamanders lay single eggs attached to leaves and stems.

Collecting spawn & tadpoles

The best place to collect spawn is from a friend's garden pond. Only collect from a 'wild' pond if there is plenty there. Remember, it takes a great many tadpoles to produce just a few frogs because so many get eaten by fish, birds and other predators.

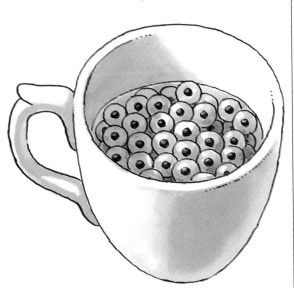

1 **Collect about a yogurt pot full of spawn or a few dozen tadpoles** using a small aquarium net. Carry them home in a small bucket. Frog spawn is the easiest to find.

2 **Put them into a small aquarium tank** (see page 64). Use tap water that has stood outside for a day or two to get rid of the chlorine. Use pond water if it is not too muddy.

3 **Add a few rocks and some water plants.** Cover the tank with netting or the birds will get a free meal.

4 **Stand the tank in dappled shade**. Tadpoles like warm water, but may die if left in full sunshine.

5 **Your tadpoles will need feeding a few days after they hatch**, unless you have a large tank with lots of water plants. At this stage they are vegetarian. Add small pieces of boiled lettuce leaves and four to five pellets of rabbit food every three or four days.

6 **Change the water if it gets murky and fill it up as it evaporates.**

Total body change

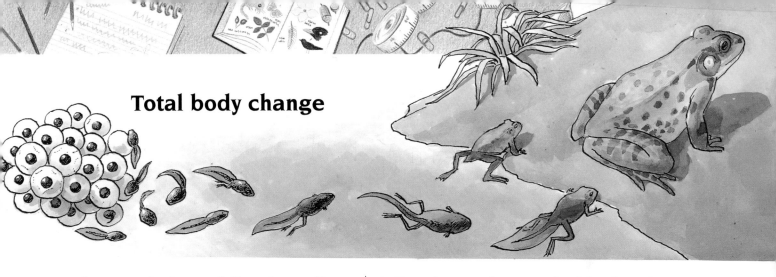

1 **Watch your tadpoles carefully** and you will see them gradually change into adults. This change is called metamorphosis. Keep a diary of what happens:
   - Can you see the gills?
   - Which comes first – hind legs or front legs?
2 **When the hind legs have appeared** (about five to six weeks after hatching), put some rocks or twigs in the tank for the tadpoles to climb out on. They will soon need to breathe air.

3 **Now they need some animal food**. So give them small pieces of raw meat, about once a week. Remove uneaten food after a couple of days and change the water twice a week.
4 **When the front legs appear**, prop up the tank so that there is a shallow end. Or you can build some islands.
5 **The small froglets or toadlets should be released** by the edge of the pond from which you took the spawn. They are very difficult to feed now, so it is better to let them go. Carry them in a box with damp moss or grass. They will drown in a bucket of water.

Marshes & Floodplains

Also called wetlands, these habitats are neither water nor really dry land. They are found mostly in lowland areas, especially where there is heavy rainfall or flooding. Wetlands that have trees growing in them are called swamps.

Bogs and marshes don't have trees. They develop in the shallows around lakes and ponds, at the edges of quiet streams, and in other low-lying areas. There is little water movement, so plants such as reeds, sedges, and water-loving grasses can grow out into the water.

These places are ideal for animals that like to spend only part of their time in the water. There are also pools for permanent water creatures such as fish. This picture shows two animals from this book; see if you can identify them.

Marsh Frog, Weatherfish.

Moor or Field Frog

This frog is pale brownish in colour with dark brown blotches. Its belly is lighter and has no markings. Like the common frog (see page 11), it has dark marks behind each eye. To help tell them apart, look for the Moor Frog's pointed snout and often striped pattern of dark on light. In the mating season, males get a bluish colour on the throat. You'll find this frog in bogs and damp meadows where it finds food such as snails, worms and insects. Groups of Moor Frogs gather around ponds in the spring. The Moor Frog hibernates in the winter, at the bottom of a pool or on dry land.

Group: Brown Frogs (Ranidae)
Size: Up to 8 cm long
Distribution: Eastern Europe, from France to Russia and Sweden

Pool Frog

This frog is similar to the marsh frog (see right), but is usually mainly green and much smaller. Sometimes it has a pale stripe down the back like the edible frog (see page 11). The backs of its thighs are usually yellowish, marbled with brown on black. It is usually found in and around small pools – hence its name – but sometimes in larger ponds and lakes.

Group: Green Frogs (Ranidae)
Size: Up to 9 cm long
Distribution: Whole of Europe, except Iberian peninsula and northern Scandinavia; only a few isolated colonies in southern Britain

This frog is rather like a large brownish version of the edible frog (see page 11). It has dark blotches, and may have green in places on its body. It has a pointed snout, and the backs of its thighs are white. Marsh Frogs live in ponds, ditches, streams and lakes. Here, they feed on insects, slugs, other frogs, lizards and sometimes small mammals such as mice. Males usually croak together in a chorus. These frogs are active during the day, and can often be seen sunbathing. In winter, they hibernate in mud at the bottom of a pool.

Group: Green Frogs (Ranidae)
Size: Up to 15 cm long
Distribution: Most of mainland Europe, but not central band from France to Italy; introduced to southern Britain

Marsh or Lake Frog

Fish

Crucian Carp

This carp has a very wide body from top to bottom. It is olive green, with a bronze tinge on the sides, and a yellowish belly. It has a scaleless head, but a fully scaled body. Its fins are dark greenish brown, except for those on its belly, which look reddish. The Crucian Carp lives in marshy pools and weedy lakes preferring almost stagnant water. Its main food is plants, but it will also eat insect larvae, crustaceans and molluscs.

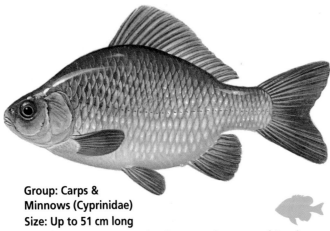

Group: Carps & Minnows (Cyprinidae)
Size: Up to 51 cm long
Distribution: Eastern England eastwards to central Russian Federation; widely introduced elsewhere

Toothcarp

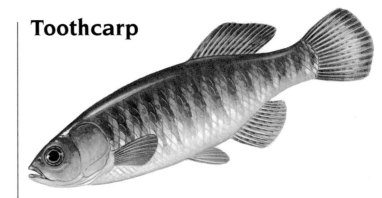

A small fish, the Toothcarp has a broad head and back. It has scales on its body, but not on its head. Its back is brownish green which fades to bronze on the lower sides and yellowish on the belly. Males have ten to fifteen brownish bands on their sides. The back and anal fins are positioned well back on its body, near its tail, which has an unforked fin. The Toothcarp lives in weedy marshes, lagoons and drainage ditches, in waters that are low in oxygen. It feeds on insect larvae and crustaceans.

Group: Toothcarps (Cyprinodontidae)
Size: Up to 6 cm long
Distribution: Along coastal area of northern Mediterranean, from France to Greece and west Turkey; a similar species is found along Spanish coast

European Mudminnow

This little fish has a stout body covered in scales. It is greenish brown above, with faint vertical bars on its sides and a yellowish belly. It lives in swamps, overgrown ponds and streams, and is one of the few fish able to tolerate low oxygen conditions in water. The European Mudminnow feeds on small insect larvae, crustaceans and molluscs.

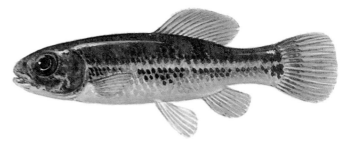

Group: Mudminnows (Umbridae)
Size: Up to 13 cm long
Distribution: Flood plain of the Danube basin running through Austria, Hungary, Romania, Czech Republic and Slovakia

Grass Carp

This big carp has a slender body with a broad, scaleless head. The rest of the body is covered in large, well-defined scales. It is dark greenish brown on its back, with pale golden sides. It lives in large rivers and swampy lakes and feeds voraciously on plant matter, even from the bank. It is very good at clearing choked waters of plants. Young Grass Carps will also eat water insect larvae and crustaceans.

Group: Carps & Minnows (Cyprinidae)
Size: Up to 1.25 m long
Distribution: Introduced to Europe

Weatherfish

Also known as the Pond Loach, this fish's trademark is a long, slender, eel-like body. It has a small head, small eyes and five pairs of barbels (whiskers) on its mouth. It is greyish brown on its back, fading to medium brown on its sides and belly. Several stripes run along its sides. The Weatherfish lives in lowland ponds and marshes, often overgrown with weeds, muddy and very low in oxygen. Few fish could cope with these conditions, but the Weatherfish rises to the surface to gulp air. It feeds on animals such as snails in the bottom mud.

Group: Loaches (Cobtidae)
Size: Up to 30 cm; usually 15 cm long
Distribution: From France, Belgium and Holland eastwards to Caspian Sea; from Denmark and Poland south to Austria

Mosquitofish

This little fish has a stout, pale-coloured body covered with noticeable scales outlined in black. There are black spots on its sides, as well as on its single back fin and its rounded tail fin. It has a small head with an upturned mouth which it uses to snatch insects from the water surface. It gets the name Mosquitofish from its preferred diet of mosquito larvae. You may see this fish in swamps, ditches, ponds, lakes, and slow-moving streams. The females do not lay eggs, but give birth to live young.

Group: Live Bearers (Poeciliidae)
Size: 5–7.5 cm long
Distribution: Southern Europe. An introduced species common in Italy and S. France

Molluscs

Marsh Snail

The Marsh Snail looks rather like the Great Pond Snail (see page 32), but with a more slender and pointed shell. The inside of the shell is always a beautiful dark violet brown or chestnut colour. There are usually criss-cross lines on the outside of its shell. Look for the Marsh Snail in marshes and in stagnant water along the edges of rivers and lakes.

Group: Pond Snails (Lymnaeidae)
Size: Up to 3.5 cm high
Distribution: Widespread in Europe

Door Snail (Balea)

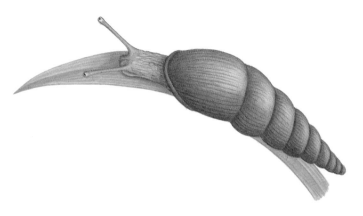

This is another snail that you will find among wet plants along river banks or in marshy and boggy areas. It does not live right in the water like the pond snails. With its long thin shell, the door snail looks more like a sea shell than a snail. The shell opening has a distinct white rim around it. There are many different sorts of door snails and not all of them live near water.

Group: Door snails (Clausiliidae)
Size: Up to about 2 cm long
Distribution: Most of Europe

Marsh Slug

You won't find any slugs in a pond unless they have fallen in by mistake! However, the Marsh Slug likes to live in very wet places like marshes and bogs. It crawls around amongst the marsh plants on which it feeds. It is a dark, pinky-brown in colour often with darker markings.

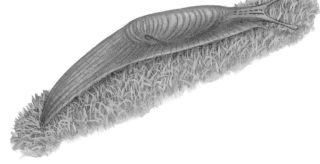

Group: Field slugs (Agriolimacidae)
Size: Up to 2.5 cm
Distribution: Throughout Europe

River Bank Snail

This snail is similar to the Marsh Snail (see right), but is larger and almost oval in shape. The shell is an almost transparent yellow colour, but may appear darker because the animal inside is dark. As its name suggests, it lives on reeds or in mud along river banks and in marshy areas. Sometimes, large numbers live together.

Group: Amber Snails (Succineidae)
Size: Up to 2 cm high
Distribution: Throughout Europe

Dwarf Pond Snail

This little snail has a shell with a short, blunt spire. The shell is brownish in colour, and its whorls are quite flattened. The animal itself is grey. You'll find the Dwarf Pond Snail in marshy places, in water meadows or in the mud around ponds, as well as in ditches. Unfortunately for the snail, it plays a part in the life-cycle of the liver fluke, a parasite that plagues sheep, cattle and sometimes people. The young larvae of the fluke swim in the water and burrow into the snail. They do not kill it, but here they multiply and change shape before leaving the snail in huge swarms. They are then eaten or drunk by sheep or cattle.

Group: Pond Snails (Lymnaeidae)
Size: 8–12 mm high
Distribution: Throughout Europe

Amber Snail

This snail does not live in the water, but is always found near it on plants along the bank. It is called 'amber' because of the yellowish colour of its shell, which is glossy and transparent. Its body is pale in colour and cannot be withdrawn completely into its shell. The Amber Snail lives in marshes among reed beds and rushes.

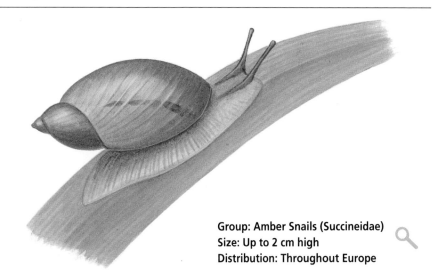

Group: Amber Snails (Succineidae)
Size: Up to 2 cm high
Distribution: Throughout Europe

What Can I Catch?

Make a minnow trap

An easy way to study fish is to catch them and take them home. This trap should catch minnows, sticklebacks or catfish.

1 **Make two cone shapes** out of wire mesh.
2 **Fix the wide open end of each one** on to a circle of stout wire.
3 **Push the narrow ends back inside** to make two smaller cones pointing inward.

4 **Cut the ends off the small cones to leave a small hole** big enough for small fish to swim through (about 5–7.5 cm across).
5 **Fix the two halves together** with a wire hinge and bulldog clip so it can be easily opened.
6 **Bait the trap** with dry dog or cat food or scraps of meat and fish. Put the bait in a fine mesh bag and hang it inside the trap.
7 **Set the trap some way out in a pond, lake or stream**. Let it drift downstream from a promontory or ask an adult to help if you need to use a boat.
8 **Anchor it with a rope** to a bush or tree and leave it for several hours or overnight.
9 **Don't forget to check it next day** or the fish will die.

Adopt a site

If you have a favourite pond, stream or swamp near you, visit it regularly (perhaps once a month) and get to know it really well. You will be able to find out which animals live there, and which are just passing through. What happens in winter and in spring? Make a plan of the site, name the different parts and mark where the animals are found. You could repeat this at different times of the year.

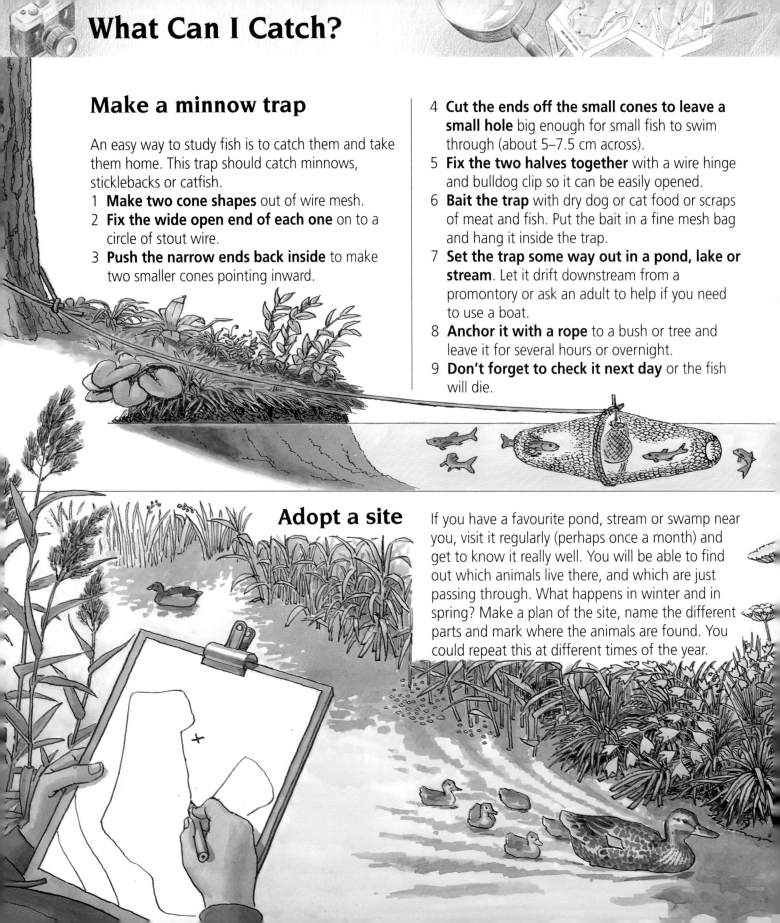

Stream bottom sampler

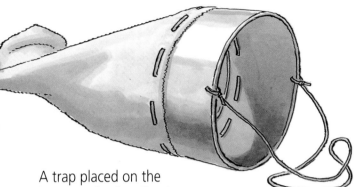

1 **Remove the bottom from a large biscuit tin** or a similar container such as a Tupperware box.
2 **Fix a fine conical net over one end**.
3 **Hold or weigh the box down on the stream bed** with the open mouth facing upstream so that the current flows through the net.
4 **Use a stick to stir up the bottom sediment and turn over stones** in front of the box. The dislodged animals will be swept through the box and into the net.

A trap placed on the bottom of a fast-flowing stream is ideal for catching the creatures that live there, as they get swept into it by the current. This is good for catching water skaters, shrimps, mayfly larvae and even small fish. **Be careful not to get too close to the edge of the water when taking your samples.**

Pollution Watch

Is your local river or stream polluted? Here are some of the signs you should look out for.

- **Water changes colour or is cloudy** (except after heavy rain)
- **Metal rubbish**: like shopping trolleys, old tyres, prams
- **Sewage**: disposable nappies, toilet paper, etc.
- **Thick, green algae** covering the surface – this is a sign of nitrogen pollution from the land
- **Bad smell** rising from the water
- **White or brown foam** on the surface
- **A line of grease** on rocks and boulders above the usual water level
- **Oil or fuel spills** – this shows up as rainbow-coloured circles floating on the surface
- **Dead fish** floating or washed up on the bank

If there is a marked change in the river or stream, alert an adult as soon as you can and get them to inform the local health officials and the National Rivers Authority. **Don't dip your equipment or your hands in the water.**

Slow Rivers & Canals

Where a river or stream reaches flat ground, its waters spread out and slow down. Mud and sand carried by the water settles out and makes a soft, muddy bottom in which many plants are able to grow. Water lilies, reeds, and sedges provide shelter for birds, fish and amphibians.

Along the river bank, look out for salamanders, frogs, and toads. Mud banks and old logs are good places to look for snakes and terrapins sunning themselves. Search along the river's edge with a dip net and you might surprise some tadpoles, or catch a stickleback.

Hiding on the bottom and among the weeds in the warm, murky water are fish, worms, snails and crayfish. Most lowland rivers are muddy, which makes it difficult to see any fish. Lowland rivers flowing through chalk areas are usually crystal clear because the chalky sediment dissolves and drops to the bottom. Clear rivers and streams are the best places to try out your viewing box (see pages 16–17). Many sorts of water snails, crayfish, and shrimps thrive in these lime-rich waters as well as a wide variety of fishes. This picture shows nine animals from this book; see how many you can identify.

Bream, Gudgeon, Spined Loach, River Pearl Mussel, Swan Mussel, Rudd, Spire Shell (Bythynia), River Snail, Wels.

Fish

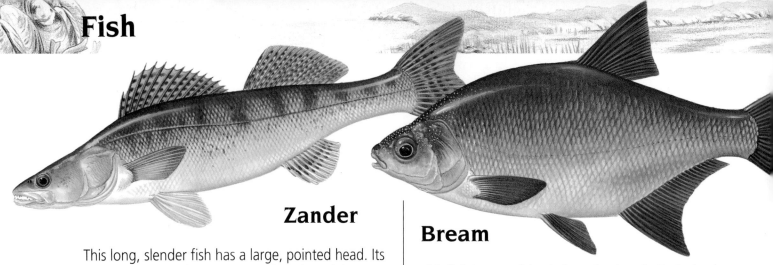

Zander

This long, slender fish has a large, pointed head. Its big mouth has a fearsome set of teeth with long fangs in the front. There are two separate back fins. The first has long, strong spines, and the second has mainly softer rays. Its back is greenish brown, fading down the sides to a white belly. There are faint dusky bars on its sides, and its back and tail fins are spotted. The Zander lives in groups in lowland rivers and lakes. When young, it feeds on insect larvae and young fish. When adult, it feeds entirely on fish, which it hunts at dawn and dusk.

Group: Perches (Percidae)
Size: Up to 1.3 m long, usually smaller
Distribution: Most of Europe; introduced to Great Britain

Bream

This fish has a tall body from back to belly. Its back is humped and is dark brown or greyish. Its sides are golden brown in adults, and silvery in young Bream. Fins are greyish brown, and its tail fin is forked. Its head, which is quite small, is scaleless, while its body is covered in small scales. The Bream lives in deep, slow-flowing rivers, lakes and ponds, where it feeds on the bottom in groups. Their food consists of worms, molluscs, crustaceans and insect larvae, all sucked up by its tube-like mouth.

Group: Carps & Minnows (Cyprinidae)
Size: Up to 50 cm, exceptionally 80 cm long
Distribution: Much of Europe, but not south of the Alps

Ide

This big fish has a fairly slender body and a broad head. It has a blunt snout and a large mouth. Its body, which is greenish brown on top and silvery on the sides and belly, is covered in small scales. Its fins are reddish, and the tail fin is forked. The Ide lives in the lower parts of large rivers, in estuaries and in deep lakes. The young feed on plankton on the surface, while older fish feed on insect larvae, crustaceans, molluscs and young fish.

A yellow version of this fish is known as the **Golden Orfe**, and can often be seen in ornamental ponds in parks and gardens.

Group: Carps & Minnows (Cyprinidae)
Size: Up to 43 cm, occasionally 100 cm long
Distribution: Southern Sweden and Germany, east to central Russian Federation: ornamental forms more widespread

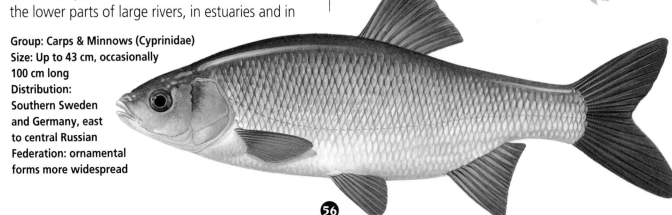

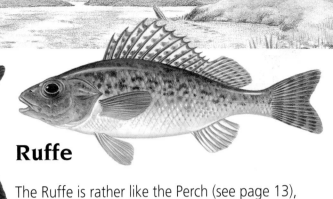

Ruffe

The Ruffe is rather like the Perch (see page 13), but the two back fins are joined together. Be careful if you handle this fish because the first part of its back fin is very spiny. The back and sides of this fish are greenish brown, spotted with a darker colour, while its lower sides are yellow and its belly is white. Its fins are yellowish, all with spots, except for the fins underneath. The Ruffe lives in muddy bottomed lakes and rivers in small groups. It feeds close to the bottom on blood worms, other small animals and fish eggs.

Group: Perches (Percidae)
Size: Usually up to 15 cm, occasionally 30 cm long
Distribution: Northern and Central Europe, but not south of the Alps

Rudd

This fish has a tall body from back to belly, and a smallish, scaleless head. The rest of its body is covered with well defined scales. It is a deep greenish brown colour on its back, with bronze sides and a creamy belly. You can tell it from the similar Roach (see page 12) because all its fins are reddish, and the tail fin is deeply forked. The Rudd lives in lowland rivers, marshes and lakes in groups. It often feeds from the water surface, a habit that is made easy by its upward-angled mouth. Its food includes insect larvae and insects, crustaceans and plant matter.

Group: Carps & Minnows (Cyprinidae)
Size: Up to 45 cm long
Distribution: Most of Europe, but not Spain and Portugal or the far north

Chub

The Chub has a rounded body with a broad head and 'shoulders'. It has a blunt snout and a wide mouth. The scales on its body are large and outlined in black, so they are easy to see. Its back is green or grey-brown, its sides silvery and its belly white. The Chub lives in rivers and occasionally in large lakes, where it feeds on insect larvae, crustaceans and small fish.

Group: Carps & Minnows (Cyprinidae)

Size: Up to 61 cm long
Distribution: Throughout Europe, except extreme north

Bleak

This slender fish has an upturned mouth with a lower jaw that sticks out, and rather large eyes. On top, the Bleak is blue-green. Its sides and belly are brilliant silver. If handled, its large scales will come off easily. There is one fin on its back, and its tail fin is forked. The Bleak lives in slow-flowing rivers, and feeds on small crustaceans and insects which it snaps from the water surface.

Group: Carps & Minnows (Cyprinidae)
Size: Up to 20 cm long – Distribution: Central and Eastern Europe, but not Spain and Portugal

Fish

Gudgeon

This fish has a slender body with a curved back and a large head. It has a greenish brown back, yellowish sides with dark blotches and a cream belly. There are large scales on its body, but its head is scaleless. Its back, tail and belly fins are covered in spots, and the tail fin is forked. A barbel (whisker) at each corner of its mouth helps it to feel for food such as insect larvae, crustaceans and molluscs along the bottom of rivers and lakes.

Group: Carps & Minnows (Cyprinidae)
Size: Up to 20 cm long
Distribution: Throughout Europe; introduced to Ireland and Spain

Spined Loach

This unusual looking fish is long and very slender. It has a small head and eyes, and its mouth has six short barbels on the lips. The name 'spined' comes from the spine under each eye, usually hidden under the skin. Its back and tail fins are rounded. The Spined Loach is light brown on its back and sides with a pattern of rounded dark patches along its sides. Its belly is creamy coloured. It uses its barbels to feel along the bottom of slow-flowing rivers and lakes for food, mainly crustaceans. Most of the time, it lies buried in the mud or sand on the bottom, or hides among the weeds.

Group: Loaches (Cobitidae)
Size: Up to 13.5 cm long
Distribution: Eastern England eastwards to Asia; from southern Sweden and Lithuania southwards to Spain, Italy and the Balkans

Wels

The Wels is a fearsome-looking catfish that hardly looks like a fish. It has a long, slender body, with a very broad head and a big mouth, framed by three pairs of barbels (whiskers). The upper two barbels are long and trail in the water. The Wels has no scales at all, and is dull brown or green on its back with some yellow mottling on its sides and cream on its belly. Its back fin is tiny compared to its big body, but the fin underneath is very long. This fish lives in slow-flowing rivers, lowland ponds and marshes often overgrown with weeds, and is active mainly by night. It feeds on bottom-dwelling fish, as well as ducklings, water voles and amphibians.

Group: European Catfishes (Siluridae)
Size: Up to 3 m; usually 1 m long
Distribution: Southern Sweden south to Rhine; along Danube and eastwards to Russian Federation; introduced to Great Britain, France, Spain and northern Italy

Burbot

This long fish has a broad, pointed head and a big mouth with a single barbel (whisker) on the chin. The fins on its back and belly run along almost half its body length. The Burbot is dull greenish brown on the back, becoming lighter and very mottled on the sides. Its belly is yellowish white. It lives in slow-flowing rivers and in lakes, hiding under tree roots, banks and among water plants. Food consists of insect larvae, crustaceans, worms and fish.

Group: Codfishes (Gadidae)
Size: Up to 1 m, usually 50 cm long
Distribution: Most of Northern Europe; now extinct in Great Britain

Freshwater Blenny

This little fish has slippery, scaleless skin. Its head is bulbous and the mouth has fleshy lips and strong teeth. It is dark brownish on its back, fading to a mottled greenish brown on the sides and cream on the belly. It has one spiny back fin which runs almost from head to tail, and the fin underneath is also long and spiny. Most blennies live in the sea, but the Freshwater Blenny lives in lakes and large rivers, particularly those with a rocky bottom. It can prop itself up on its two front fins, using them like stilts. It feeds on crustaceans, insect larvae and sometimes on small fish.

Group: Blennies (Blenniidae)
Size: Up to 15 cm; usually 6–8 cm long
Distribution: Coasts of Spain, southern France, Italy, Greece and Turkey

Sterlet

With its long body, pointed tail and long snout, this fish is easy to recognize. Instead of scales, the Sterlet has rows of bony plates on its body. Its snout has four fringed barbels (whiskers) attached to it. The Sterlet has a greyish brown back, fading down the sides to a yellowish belly. The plates along its sides are light in colour. It lives in large rivers close to the river-bed over gravelly bottoms. Like all sturgeon, it is much rarer than it was. Its food consists of insect larvae, molluscs, worms and leeches.

Group: Sturgeons (Acipenseridae)
Size: Up to 1.25 m long
Distribution: Eastern Europe, mainly in rivers connected to the Black, Caspian and White Seas

Fish Found in Estuaries

Mullet

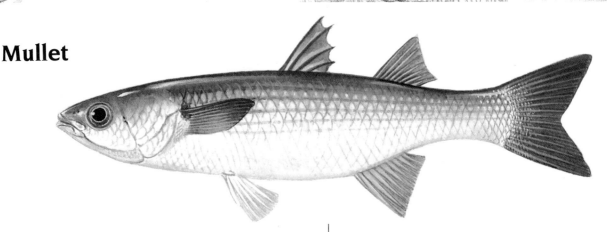

Mullet have a torpedo-shaped body with a wide head, large eyes and a broad, rounded back. There are two separate back fins. The first has four strong spines, and the second has rays. Mullet are grey-blue above, and silvery on the sides with faint grey stripes and white on the belly. Mullet live in bays, estuaries and the lower parts of rivers where the water is not very salty, and sometimes in fresh water. They feed on algae and suck crustaceans and worms from the bottom mud.

Group: Grey Mullets (Mugilidae) – Size: Up to 60 cm long
Distribution: European coastal waters

Smelt

This fish looks a bit like a very small salmon. Like salmon, it has one proper fin on the back and a small, fleshy fin, called an 'adipose' fin, near the tail. It is light olive-brown on its back, silvery on its sides and creamy-white on its belly. There is also a silvery line on its sides. Its jaws are big with sharp teeth, and its tail fin is sharply forked. The Smelt breeds in gravel-bottomed rivers in winter and early spring. When the eggs hatch in the autumn, the young swim down to estuaries and the sea. The Smelt feeds on crustaceans in the plankton, and on small fish.

Group: Smelts (Osmeridae)
Size: Up to 30 cm long, usually smaller
Distribution: West coast of Europe from Norway to north Spain, including Baltic Sea

Sandsmelt

Small and slender, the Sandsmelt is greenish on its back, and silvery-white below. There is a bright silvery stripe along each of its sides. Its head is small, with an upward-pointing mouth, but its eyes are large. There are two separate fins on its back, the first with flexible spines. Its tail is forked. The Sandsmelt lives in coastal waters and in salty lakes and lagoons. It swims in big, tightly packed groups, feeding on small crustaceans, worms, molluscs and young fish.

Group: Sandsmelts (Antherinidae)
Size: Up to 9 cm long – Distribution: Most European coasts

Common Goby

This little Goby has a stout body, a broad head, thick lips and bulbous eyes. Like all gobies, it has two fins on its back, the first of which is spiny. The second fin has soft rays, and the tail fin is rounded. The Common Goby is light greyish brown on its back, fading to a cream belly. Its sides are speckled with dark blotches, and adult males have vertical dark bars on their sides. This fish lives in estuaries, on muddy coastal marshes, and in the sea. It feeds on small crustaceans, worms, midge larvae and mites.

Group: Gobies (Gobiidae)
Size: Up to 6.5 cm long
Distribution: Most of coastal Europe

Bass

The Bass has a torpedo-shaped body and a large head. There are two separate fins on its back. The first has long, slender spines, and the second has rays. Its tail fin is slightly forked. All of its body and part of its head is covered in scales. Its head is pointed, and its mouth is large. This fish is greenish grey on its back, and brilliant silver on its sides and belly. It lives in coastal waters and estuaries. It is more likely that you will see young Bass in estuaries, which they use as nursery grounds. In rivers, the Bass feeds on small crustaceans and young fish. On the coast, it feeds on crustaceans, fish and squid.

Group: Sea Basses (Serranidae)
Size: Up to 1 m; usually about 60 cm long
Distribution: European coastal waters and estuaries

Flounder

The Flounder is a typical flatfish, with both eyes on the same side of its head. It lies flat on the sea- or river-bed, and doesn't swim from side to side like other fish, but with an up and down, wave-like movement. The Flounder is mottled brown on its back and white underneath. It breeds in shallow water on the coast, then the young fish migrate into rivers, where they settle on the river-bed. Flounders feed on bottom-dwelling crustaceans, insect larvae, worms and molluscs. It is the only flatfish found in fresh water in Europe.

Group: Right-eyed Flatfishes (Pleuronectidae)
Size: Up to 51 cm long in the sea; up to 20 cm in fresh water
Distribution: Widespread in the sea; only northern Europe in fresh water

Molluscs & Crustaceans

River Snail

The River Snail is one of the bigger freshwater snails. It is easily recognized by its rounded, greenish brown shell, which has about five fat whorls, each with broad, dark bands. The River Snail can survive for a time out of water because it can seal itself into its shell with a shell door called an 'operculum', and so can keep its gills wet. It lives in slow-flowing rivers, and gives birth to live young rather than laying eggs like many other snails. Its young are unusual – they have hairy shells!

Group: Freshwater Winkles (Viviparidae)
Size: Up to 4 cm high
Distribution: Throughout Europe
except most northerly or southerly parts

Common Valve Snail

The brownish, rounded shell of this snail has a low spire shaped rather like a lady's hair bun. It can close the shell opening with a distinctive coiled 'operculum' (shell door). In live specimens, look for the animal's characteristic blunt snout. You should find it in thick weed along the river's edge.

Group: Valve Snails (Valvidae)
Size: Up to 7 mm high
Distribution: Widespread in Europe

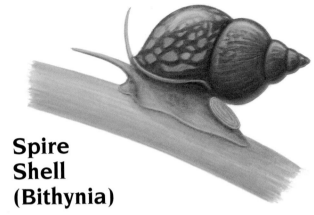

Spire Shell (Bithynia)

This snail is similar to the Jenkin's Spire Shell (see below), but it is larger. The shell is pale brown often with darker blotches. The animal inside is greyish in colour. The Spire Shell lives in rivers, canals and ditches, and can seal itself in using its hard 'operculum' (shell door). It lays eggs in jelly-like capsules.

Group: Spire Shells (Bithyniidae)
Size: Up to 1.5 cm high – Distribution: Widespread in Europe

Jenkin's Spire Shell

These tiny brown or blackish snails with their tall, pointed spires, can be found in their hundreds on the muddy banks of rivers, in canals, in estuaries and on muddy sea shores. It is only during the last one hundred years that this snail has moved up from the sea to live in fresh water – an interesting example of an animal that we can observe as it evolves and colonizes a new habitat.

Group: Spire Shells (Hydrobidae)
Size: Up to 5 mm high
Distribution: Most of Europe

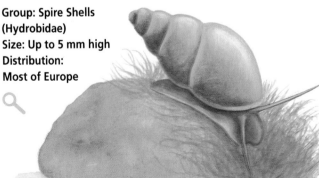

Amphipod (Corophium)

This little animal is like the Freshwater shrimp found in clean streams and rivers (see page 73). You can tell them apart because the Amphipod is much smaller and has short fat antennae. It can also live in much muddier places including estuaries, slow rivers and canals. It lives in a flimsy tube built from mucus and rubbish.

Group: Amphipods (Amphipoda)
Size: up to 6 mm – Distribution: Most of Europe

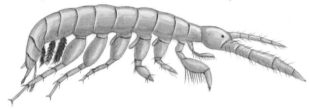

Mitten Crab

Most crabs live in salt water in the sea. The Mitten Crab is found in rivers, but it has to return to the sea to breed. So it is only found in rivers connecting with the sea. It is easy to recognize because it has dense fur covering the claws. In some places it is a pest because it makes holes in the river banks causing them to collapse.

Group: Crabs (Decapod crustaceans) – Size: Up to 6 cm
Distribution: Introduced to Germany from Asia. Now also in Great Britain, Scandinavia, Holland, Belgium and France.

Painter's Mussel

This mussel has two oval-shaped shells, which are yellowish green to brown in colour. It prefers quiet water in rivers, streams, lakes and reservoirs with muddy bottoms. Here it lies partly buried, with its siphons sticking out, filtering food from the water. The larvae or young mussels attach themselves to the skin of fish and feed off them for the first few weeks of their lives. When they are ready, they drop off the fish and start their lives independently.

Group: Freshwater Mussels (Unionidae)
Size: Up to 15 cm across – Distribution: Most of Europe

Swan Mussel

Many sorts of mussel live in fresh water and it can be difficult to tell them apart. The Swan Mussel is one of the largest. It has an oval shell flattened on one side. Yellowish green to olive-brown is their normal colour, but they are often stained a dirty black. In contrast, the inside of the shell is a lovely, iridescent mother-of-pearl. It lives in ponds, canals, and slow-flowing rivers. Food is filtered from the water as it lies half-buried in the mud.

Group: Freshwater Mussels (Unionidae)
Size: Up to 15 cm across
Distribution: Throughout Europe

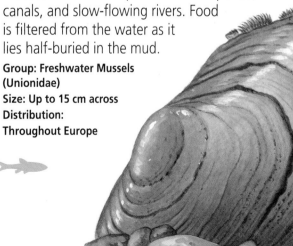

Keep Them at Home

It's easy to make your own temporary aquarium, using water and creatures from the pond. Keeping it at home will let you study your water creatures every day, and chart their progress. Use this book to help you identify the animals you find and make a list of them.

Repeat this at regular intervals. You will find that new animals magically appear. They have hatched out of tiny eggs or changed from larvae into adults.

Most pond animals develop from eggs laid by the adults which hatch into larvae. The larvae are usually very different from the adults. Sometimes the adults live in the pond as well, for example diving beetles. Sometimes they live on land, for example dragonflies. With a bit of patience, you can find out which animals have laid eggs in your aquarium.

Make an aquarium

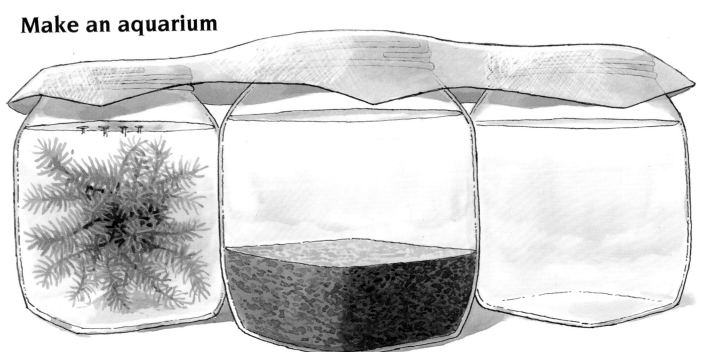

1 **Buy three cheap plastic aquaria** at your local pet shop, or else use large sweet jars or Tupperware boxes. If you use sweet jars, they must have wide openings to allow plenty of oxygen in.

2 **Half-fill the first container with pond weed** and fill it up with pond water.

3 **In the second one, put a good layer of mud** from the bottom of the pond and fill up with pond water.

4 **Fill the third container with pond water only.** Put the containers outside in the shade and cover them with netting.

5 **Look into the containers after a day** to see what has crawled out of the weed and mud. Find out which of your containers has the widest variety of animals.

6 **Your aquaria should last for several weeks** provided they are kept cool and there is a large enough surface of water in contact with the air.

Caddisfly cases

If you find caddisfly cases with the larvae still in them, you can watch how they build their home. Each caddis case is open at both ends to allow a flow of water through it.

1 **If you push a toothpick very gently into the narrow end of the case,** the caddisfly larva will come out as it does not like being tickled! Now you can see it clearly. It will go back inside given the chance.

2 **Take away its old case** and keep the larva in a plastic box or jar in a cool, shady place, filled with the pond water that you found it in.
3 **Put in some tiny coloured beads**, and it will rebuild its home out of these.

4 **Or you can give it pieces of the material** it normally uses, such as twigs, or shells, and watch it rebuild its home.
5 **It's best to try this experiment with several caddisfly larvae**, in case one of them is lazy.

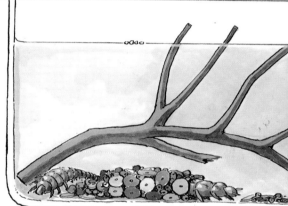

The somersaulting hydra

A hydra is a small animal that is up to about 1.5 cm long when expanded (see page 42). It looks like a hollow tube with a ring of tentacles at one end surrounding the mouth, and can move slowly by turning somersaults!

1 **Find a pond or ditch where there is a carpet of duckweed** on the surface or many floating water lily leaves.

2 **Collect water lily leaves** and look on the underside for blobs of jelly.
3 **Lift off these blobs with your paintbrush**, and leave them in water in a jar. If they are hydra, they will soon expand.
4 **Collect a quantity of duckweed**, and put it into a large jar of pond water. Keep it until the next day. Look at the sides of the jar for hydra. Watch them. They might somersault for you.

Fast Streams & Rivers

Many rivers begin life far up in the hills or mountains. Sweeping away mud or sand, the swift current runs over boulders, stones and gravel. On steep downhill sections, there will be waterfalls and rapids. The rushing water provides plenty of oxygen, but the animals living here must be tough enough to prevent themselves being washed away.

Many insect larvae can live here. Look for the flattened nymphs of mayflies and stoneflies clinging under stones. Some caddisfly larvae anchor themselves to the bottom in silken nets. Wet boulders are favoured by black fly larvae which have hooks to cling on with. If you are on holiday in Europe, look for the fire salamander which feeds on the insect larvae hiding beneath stones.

Few snails are found in fast waters, but river pearl mussels dig into the stream bed and rely on a current to bring them food. Crayfish cling to the sides of rocks with their strong legs and claws. Small fish like bullhead are flattened on their lower side and are streamlined. They lie with their head pointing upstream so that the water flows over them. Trout and salmon are also streamlined and are powerful swimmers.

Other animals are fussy about temperature and will live only in cold waters. This means they are found only in northern and mountain areas where water temperatures in large lakes and rivers remain low all the year round. Some of these are shown on pages 76–77. This picture shows seven animals from this book; see how many you can identify.

Crayfish, Brook Lamprey, River Limpets, Stone Loach, Miller's Thumb (fish), Fire Salamander, Bladder Snail.

Atlantic Salmon

You can recognize all salmon and trout by their streamlined shape and small, fleshy second back fin. Most salmon have a slightly forked tail, whereas in trout, it is almost straight. Adult Atlantic Salmon are silvery with a few scattered spots (below). During the breeding season, the male develops red spots and a reddish belly. His lower jaw grows forward into a hooked shape. The Atlantic Salmon leads a complex life. It spends most of its life in the sea, but returns to the stream in which it hatched in order to breed. It will struggle up waterfalls and rapids to get there. After spawning, some die, but many return to the sea and will later spawn again. The young, or parr, are quite dark and have blotchy sides. At two to six years old, they start to move downstream, become silvery, and are called smolts.

Group: Trout & Salmon (Salmonidae)
Size: Up to 1.4 m long – Distribution: Northern European coastal waters, as far south as northern Portugal

Rainbow Trout

This fish gets its name from its beautiful rainbow of blue, green, and pink that covers its body (above). Its body, tail, and back fin are also heavily speckled with small, dense black spots. Rainbow Trout live mostly in artificial waters including lakes and reservoirs. They can also be found in streams and rivers. They do not breed well in Europe and are mostly reared in hatcheries and then released. The Rainbow Trout is one of the fish most sought after by anglers.

Group: Trout & Salmon (Salmonidae)
Size: Up to 1.2 m long
Distribution: Introduced widely in Europe

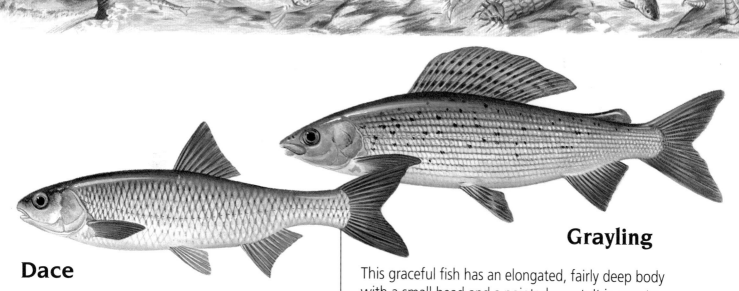

Grayling

This graceful fish has an elongated, fairly deep body with a small head and a pointed snout. It is easy to recognize from its spectacular, tall, dorsal fin. There is also a small fleshy, 'adipose' fin near its tail. It is has a steel-blue to greenish brown back and silvery sides with faint violet stripes. The scales are big and easy to see. Its back fin is high with many rays, and bears rows of spots. The tail fin itself is forked. The Grayling lives in clean, cool rivers and mountain lakes. It feeds on insect larvae, crustaceans and molluscs that live on the bottom.

Group: Graylings (Thymallidae)
Size: Up to 50 cm long
Distribution: Northwestern Europe, south to the Alps

Dace

This slim-bodied fish has a small head and mouth. On top, it is greenish olive, fading to bright silver on its sides and white on its belly. There is one grey fin on its back, while the fins on its sides and underneath have a yellowish orange tinge. Its tail fin is forked. The Dace lives in groups in clean, fast-flowing rivers, feeding on crustaceans, flying insects and their water-dwelling larvae.

Group: Carps and Minnows (Cyprinidae)
Size: Up to 25 cm long
Distribution: Most of Europe, but not Spain or south of the Alps

Brown Trout

This trout is greeny-brown with silvery sides and is speckled with large, dark spots. It also has scattered red spots faintly surrounded by blue. Unlike the rainbow trout, it has an unspotted tail. The Brown Trout lives in moderately fast rivers and streams, often hiding in quiet pools and also in lakes. However some Brown Trout migrate to the sea, when they are called Sea Trout. Brown Trout become most active at dusk, when they will 'rise' to snap up surface insects. They also feed on molluscs, crustaceans, and even smaller Brown Trout.

Group: Trout & Salmon (Salmonidae)
Size: Up to 1 m long
Distribution: Throughout Europe

Bullhead

Also known as the Miller's Thumb, this strange-looking little fish has a tapering body with a broad, flattened head and a very wide mouth. There is a short spine on each gill cover, and two fins on its back, the second longer than the first. The Bullhead is a mottled, dark, greenish brown with dark blotches, and has a pale belly. It can vary its colour to some extent, to match its background. It lives in streams, usually hiding under stones or among plants, and becomes active at night. Its food consists of crustaceans, insect larvae, and salmon and trout eggs. Males guard the eggs, which are laid under stones in the spring.

Group: Bullheads (Cottidae)
Size: Up to 8 cm long
Distribution: Most of Europe

Stone Loach

This slender, rounded fish has a large head with small, high-set eyes and six long barbels (whiskers) around its mouth. On top, it is greenish brown, fading to yellowish on its sides and belly. Its sides are covered with dusky blotches which help it to hide among gravel and stones. There is one short fin on its back and the tail fin is not forked. The Stone Loach lives in small streams and rivers, and probably got its name from its habit of hiding under stones. If you can catch one, it will make a good aquarium pet. It feeds on bottom-dwelling crustaceans, insect larvae and worms.

Group: Loaches (Cobitidae)
Size: Up to 15 cm long
Distribution: Most of Europe, but not the far north or south of the Alps

Minnow

This little fish is familiar to many people and has at least sixteen other names in Britain alone! It has a rounded body and a blunt head. It is olive-brown on top and creamy on its belly. Its sides have a row of dusky blotches or sometimes a dark stripe. In the spring breeding season, the males have red bellies and black throats. You can catch minnows in most small, fast streams, but they also live in rivers, lakes and reservoirs where there are gravel patches for them to lay their eggs in.

Group: Carps & Minnows (Cyprinidae)
Size: Up to 8 cm long
Distribution: Most of Europe, but not Spain and Portugal

Brook Lamprey

The Brook Lamprey looks like a snake or an eel. It has a long body with a sucker disc instead of jaws. On each side of its head, seven gill openings are visible. Two fins on its back lie together on the end of its body. The Brook Lamprey is greenish brown on its back, which fades to yellowish sides, and has a cream belly. Lamprey larvae live buried in the mud in rivers, filtering food out of their muddy home. The adults do not feed at all.

Group: Lampreys (Petromyzontidae)
Size: Up to 25 cm long
Distribution: Northwestern Europe from Ireland east to Finland, and south to central France

Barbel

With its long, slender body and golden colouring, this is a striking-looking fish. The Barbel has a pointed, scaleless head, and thick lips with two pairs of fleshy 'barbels' (whiskers) hanging below its mouth. Its back is greenish brown, fading to bright golden brown on its sides. Its brown, single, back fin is high and has a serrated spine. Its tail fin is forked and its belly fins are yellowish orange. The Barbel lives on the bottom gravel of large, clear lowland rivers. It feeds on bottom-dwelling crustaceans, insect larvae and molluscs, which it locates with the help of its mouth barbels.

Group: Carps & Minnows (Cyprinidae)
Size: Up to 60 cm, sometimes 90 cm long
Distribution: Widespread in Europe, but not northern parts including Scotland

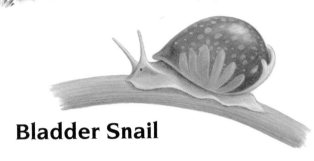

Bladder Snail

This snail has an unusual shell. It is bulbous and fragile, with a short, blunt spire. It is pale brown in colour, and almost transparent. It is also very glossy, because the animal inside wraps part of itself around its shell when it is out and 'polishes' it. The animal itself is pale to dark grey. The Bladder Snail lives in fast-flowing rivers where there are lots of plants.

Group: Bladder Snails (Physidae)
Size: Up to 12 mm long – Distribution: Most of Europe

River Pearl Mussel

This mussel lives on sandy bottoms of cool, clear streams and small rivers. Its thick, heavy shell is yellow-brown when young, then the colour changes to dark brown to black when it gets older. Inside, its shell is pearly white. Sometimes the River Pearl Mussel forms small pearls. Like some other mussels, the newly-hatched young attach themselves to fish and feed off them for a few weeks. They grow very slowly and can live to be ninety years old!

Group: Pearly Mussels (Margaritiferidae)
Size: 7.5–15 cm – Distribution: Throughout Europe

Nerite

This snail's thick shell is patterned with irregular brown to violet markings. Underneath, it has a big D-shaped opening. It lives mostly on stones in rivers, but may also be seen in canals and lakes. This snail can seal the opening of its shell with a hard cover, called an 'operculum'. Its eggs are laid in horny capsules.

Group: Nerites (Neritidae)
Size: Up to 12 mm long
Distribution:
Most of Europe

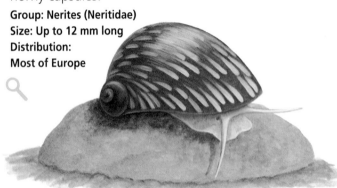

River Limpet

This limpet lives in fast-flowing streams, on the shores of large lakes, and in large springs where it clings on to rocks and stones. Its shell is taller than the Lake Limpet (see page 33) and cone-shaped, with a spire that curves back to the right. In colour it varies from greyish to reddish brown.

Group: Freshwater Limpets (Ancylidae)
Size: Up to 8 mm long
Distribution:
Most of Europe

Freshwater Shrimp

Freshwater Shrimps resemble the sand hoppers and beach fleas that you find on the seashore. They are flattened sideways and curved into an arc shape. There are several different species which vary in colour from grey to greenish or orange-brown. You will not find them in stagnant ponds, but they are common in almost any clean, running water and in large lakes. Fish love to eat them, so they hide under stones and among plants. They eat decaying plants and animals.

Group: Amphipods (Amphipoda)
Size: Up to 2.5 cm long – Distribution: Most of Europe

European Crayfish

Also known as the Noble Crayfish, this is the commonest species in continental Europe. It is not easy to tell it apart from the White-footed Crayfish (see above), but it is often more reddish in colour and grows to a larger size. In France and many other countries, it is a much-prized delicacy and is boiled and eaten. Like true lobsters, it turns red when cooked.

Group: Crayfishes (Astacidae)
Size: Up to 15 cm long
Distribution: Northern Europe, from Scandinavia and France to eastern Europe, but not Great Britain

White-footed Crayfish

A crayfish is like a very small lobster, but it lives in fresh water instead of the sea. Two large claws at the front are used to catch and eat small animals including fish. There are four other pairs of legs with which it walks, but it can also jet quickly backwards using its tail fan. The White-footed Crayfish is yellowish brown with pale undersides to its legs.

Group: Crayfishes (Astacidae) – Size: Up to 12 cm long
Distribution: Northern Europe, but mainly France, Belgium and Great Britain

Signal Crayfish

This is an American species that has been introduced to Europe. This was done because it is immune to a fungal disease that has killed large numbers of European Crayfish and White-footed Crayfish (see opposite). It is brown in colour with a whitish spot on the hinge of its claw, that gives it its name. Unfortunately in some areas, including Britain, the native crayfish are being pushed out by this and other introduced species.

Group: Crayfishes (Astacidae)
Size: Up to 15 cm long
Distribution: Great Britain, Sweden, Finland and other scattered localities

Black Fly Larva

Swarms of tiny, biting Black Flies can be enough to spoil a summer picnic. The young of these annoying flies cover rocks and plants in small, fast-flowing streams. Look carefully at the tops of rocks and around waterfalls and you are bound to see them. They fix themselves to the rock by a pad of silk into which they lock their tail end. They strain food from the water with two foldable fans of bristles.

Group: Black Flies (Simuliidae)
Size: Up to 7 mm long
Distribution:
Throughout
Europe

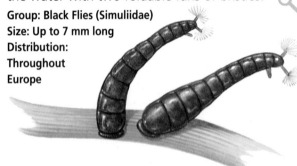

Caddisfly Larva (Hydropsyche)

Adult caddisflies look like small moths and live on land. The larvae look rather like caterpillars and live in the water. Most make themselves a case; however, the Hydropsyche species acts rather like a spider. It lives in fast-running water and, instead of a case, it spins a funnel-shaped net of silk under a stone. Small animals are swept into it and eaten. If you look down into a clear stream, you might see crescent-shaped objects on the stream bed – these are the entrances to the silken nets.

Group: Caddisflies (Hydropsyche) – Size: Up to 2 cm long
Distribution: Throughout Europe

Caddisfly Larva (Rhyacophila)

Not all caddisfly larvae make cases for themselves. This larva is greenish or yellowish with tufts of gills running along the sides of its body. It spends its time creeping along under stones in streams, and hunting for food, which consists of larvae of other insects.

Group: Caddis and Sedgeflies (Tricoptera)
Size: Up to 2 cm long
Distribution: Widespread in Europe

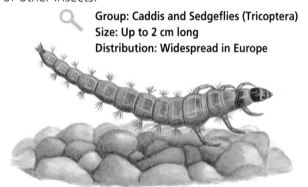

Caddisfly Larva (Agapetus)

Most caddisfly larvae build themselves a case of twigs or stones to live in. Find out how to watch them doing it on page 65. The Agapetus caddisfly larva makes a case out of sand grains and small pebbles, with an opening at each end. Look out for this larva and its case on the undersides of stones in small, fast-flowing streams in the spring.

Group: Caddis and Sedgeflies (Tricoptera)
Size: Case up to 1 cm long
Distribution: Widespread in Europe

Mayfly Nymph

There are many different kinds of mayflies, but all of them live near water. The nymph (or young) live under water mostly in streams, rivers and large lakes. Although different species vary in size and shape, all mayfly nymphs have a row of feathery or plate-like gills along the sides of the body, and three thin tails. Most are brownish in colour. The one shown here has short, sturdy legs and burrows into gravelly mud. Others cling beneath stones along with stonefly nymphs (see opposite).

Group: Mayflies (Ephemeroptera)
Size: Up to 2.5 cm long
Distribution: Throughout Europe

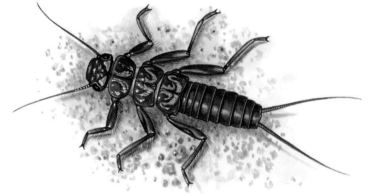

Stonefly Nymph

Like many other waterside insects, the Stonefly hatches out as a nymph that lives under water. Also known as 'creepers', the nymphs have strong legs for clinging beneath stones in the fast currents of the streams in which most species live. A pair of long antennae and two thin tails called 'cerci' will help you to distinguish them from mayfly nymphs (see opposite) with which they are often found. Although usually plain brown, some species have beautiful patterns.

Group: Stoneflies (Plecoptera)
Size: Up to 2.5 cm long
Distribution: Throughout Europe

Fish Leech (Pisicola)

As the name suggests, this leech feeds on fish. Its body is cylinder-shaped, with big suckers. It is greenish, yellowish, or brown, and may have white spots. When hungry, it 'fishes' from a rock, waving about until a fish passes. Then it lets go and swims fast until it catches the fish and clamps tightly on to it. After sucking its blood, the leech lets go and hides among the plants. If you get one in your net, it will be easy to spot as it will loop rapidly about. These leeches are found wherever there are fish.

Group: Leeches (Hirudinea) – Size: Up to 5 cm long
Distribution: Throughout Europe

Alpine Newt

The vivid colours of Alpine Newt makes it easy to recognize. Both males and females are dark grey on top with many small spots on the sides. The belly is bright orange and unspotted. Males may have bright blue sides especially in the breeding season, when they also develop a low crest. Although they may hibernate on dry land in winter, Alpine Newts spend most of their time in the water. They live mostly in forest pools, and in lakes and slow streams in mountainous areas. A wide variety of crustaceans, insects, larvae, worms and slugs is eaten. **Don't handle these newts** as they secrete a nasty substance from their skin.

Group: Salamanders & Newts (Salamandridae)
Size: Up to 12 cm long
Distribution: Central Europe, from France almost to Russia and from Denmark to northern Italy and Greece

Stream Frog

This frog is rather like the common frog (see page 11) and has a similar dark patch behind each eye. It is variable in colour, but is usually greyish. Unlike the common frog, it has a dark throat with a pale patch in the centre, and is much less widespread. It prefers mountainous areas, where it lives near cool streams. You'll see it from spring until autumn, when it hibernates buried in the soil on the forest floor, or under a pile of leaves. In the spring, the Stream Frog breeds in the water. Its food includes insects, slugs and worms.

Group: Brown Frogs (Ranidae)
Size: Up to 7.5 cm long
Distribution: Only in Italy and the Balkans from Yugoslavia south to Greece

Fire Salamander

Group: Salamanders & Newts (Salamandridae)
Size: Up to 28 cm long
Distribution: Central and southern Europe; not Great Britain

This salamander is hard to miss. It is one of the biggest and brightest amphibians in Europe. Its striking colours consist of a black background with blotches of bright yellow. These act as warning colours which help to keep enemies at bay. The Fire Salamander lives in damp wooded areas near to water. It is active by night, when it comes out to find snails, slugs, worms and insects to feed on. Females lay eggs in cool forest streams and pools, which hatch into tadpoles (see page 25). In high mountain areas, females may produce live young instead of eggs. Fire Salamanders hibernate in the winter, hiding in piles of stones or caves. **Don't touch one,** as if disturbed, these salamanders give out a poisonous secretion.

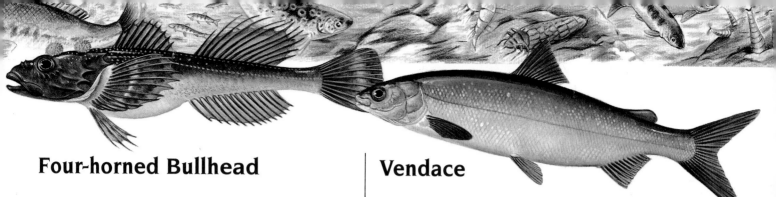

Four-horned Bullhead

The Four-horned Bullhead is easy to recognize. It has a slender body and tail, but a broad, flattened head. There are four sharp spines on each gill cover, and four lumps on top of its head. These are light coloured and spongy when the fish is living in fresh water. The two fins on its dark brown back are separate, and the second one has very long rays sticking up. It lives on the bottom of cold, freshwater lakes, and in the sea. It feeds on small bottom-living creatures.

Group: Bullheads (Cottidae) – Size: Up to 36 cm long
Distribution: Deep Baltic freshwater lakes and the Baltic Sea; in the sea on Arctic coasts of northern Europe

Vendace

The Vendace belongs to a group of fish called the whitefishes. There are many different sorts and even the experts cannot always tell them apart! Whitefish are shaped like salmon and trout. Like them, they have one fin in the middle of the back and a small, fleshy, 'adipose' fin near the tail. All whitefish have large scales and never have any spots or other colour patterns. The Vendace is a silvery fish with a greenish-blue back. It lives in large, cold lakes and sometimes in rivers.

Group: Salmon & Trout (Salmonidae)
Size: Up to 35 cm long
Distribution: Northwestern Europe, including Great Britain

Brook Charr

Brook Charr belong to the trout family and are shaped like them, with a small, fleshy 'adipose' fin and small scales. It has a very long jaw that reaches well past its eye. The olive-green to brown back and lighter sides are beautifully patterned with cream spots that run together into wavy lines. The Brook Charr lives in cold streams and lakes, feeding on insects, insect larvae and crustaceans. It is a native to the east of North America, but has been introduced to many lakes in Europe.

Group: Salmon & Trout (Salmonidae)
Size: Up to 45 cm long – Distribution: Cold European lakes

Arctic Charr

The Arctic Charr is like to the brook charr (see above), but has a smaller jaw which only just reaches past its eye. In the far north, this fish lives in rivers, and migrates to the sea in winter. This type is steel-blue on top, silvery with reddish or pink spots on its sides, and has an orange-red belly. Further south, they live in deep mountain lakes. This type is greenish brown with reddish and white spots on its sides, and also has an orange-red belly. Both forms have white edges to their fins, and a forked tail.

Group: Salmon & Trout (Salmonidae)
Size: Up to 30 cm long in lakes; up to 1 m for sea-migrants
Distribution: Arctic; cold and mountain lakes of central Europe

Find Out Some More

Useful Organizations

The best organization for you to get in touch with is your local County Wildlife Trust. There are forty-seven of these trusts in Great Britain and you should contact them if you want to know about wildlife and nature reserves and activities in your area. Ask your local library for their address, or contact:

The Wildlife Trusts (previously the Royal Society for Nature Conservation), The Green, Witham Park, Waterside South, Lincoln, LN5 7JR (01522–544400).

Wildlife Watch is the junior branch of The Wildlife Trusts. Local Wildlife Watch groups run meetings all over the country. Again you can find out about your nearest Wildlife Watch group by contacting The Wildlife Trusts.

Your local **natural history society** may organize visits to local rivers or lakes to find and study the animals and plants. They are led by local experts and you will find them of great help. Your local library will have a list of them.

National Trust for Places of Historic Interest or Natural Beauty, 36 Queen Anne's Gate, London SW1H 9AS (0171–222 9251). They own more than 570 properties and over 232,000 hectares of countryside throughout England, Wales and Northern Ireland. These include many woods, nature reserves and sites of special scientific interest. Most of this is open to visitors, but you usually have to pay to get into a property. The National Trust also run many courses with school groups; ask your teacher to find out about these.

In Scotland, contact **National Trust for Scotland** (care of the Education Adviser), 5 Charlotte Square, Edinburgh EH2 4DU (0131–226 5922).

English Nature (the Nature Conservancy Council for England), Northminster House, Peterborough, Cambs PE1 1UA. (01733–340345) They will send you a list of local nature reserves.

Many of these reserves have an interpretive centre to explain the wildlife present there.

In Scotland, contact **Scottish National Heritage**, 12 Hope Terrace, Edinburgh EH9 2AS. (0131–447 4784)

The British Trust for Conservation Volunteers (BTCV), 36 St Mary's Street, Wallingford, Oxon OX10 0EU (01491–39766). They work in partnership with landowner, local communities, councils, businesses and charities to protect and maintain rare habitats, footpaths and nature trails. They publish a quarterly magazine, called *The Conserver*, which keeps members up to date with the latest news. They also have a School Membership Scheme; ask your teacher to find out about this.

Useful Books

Create Your Own Nature Reserve, Janet Kelly (Simon & Schuster). A practical activity book that shows you how to create a nature reserve in your own garden.

Enjoying Wildlife, a guide to RSPB nature reserves, Bob Scott. Updated regularly, this tells you how to find the RSPB's nature reserves around Great Britain, and what you might see there.

Lakes, Rivers, Streams and Ponds of Britain and North-West Europe Richard Fitter and Richard Manuel (HarperCollins PHOTO GUIDES). Identification guide with many colour photos of everything from plants to mammals.

Nature Atlas of Great Britain (Pan/Ordinance Survey).

The Pocket Guide to Freshwater Fishes of Britain and Europe Alwyne Wheeler, illustrated by Colin Newman (Dragon's World). Spiral-bound guide showing more than 130 fishes.

The Pocket Guide to Insects of the Northern Hemisphere George C. McGavin, illustrated by Richard Lewington (Dragon's World).

Index & Glossary

Places To Visit

Almost every area of fresh water, ranging from a little stream to a deep lake, or from a rain butt in your garden to a slow-flowing canal will contain many different forms of wildlife. It is up to you to go and find them. Areas of freshwater that might be particularly worth a look are:

The Broads in Norfolk: they include rivers, large still lakes (the Broads themselves) and some brackish (partly salty) estuaries near the coast.

The Lake District in Cumbria: here you will find the contrast between the fast-flowing streams tumbling down from the fells and the large, cold, deep lakes themselves.

The Levels in Somerset: the very low-lying area between the Mendip Hills and the Quantock Hills. Areas of marsh with many drains and ditches.

The Highlands of Scotland: includes rivers where you might see wild salmon and land-locked tarns.

Index & Glossary